SECRETS
OF TOP
Luxury
AGENTS

MICHAEL LaFIDO

Secrets of Top Luxury Agents
Copyright © 2024

In this one of a kind book, Renowned luxury real estate expert, and founder of the LUXE Designation Michael LaFido unveils an unparalleled collaboration, gathering insights from 23 luminaries in the field and 3 rising stars, making their expertise more accessible than ever before. Discover the closely guarded secrets that have propelled these icons to the top of the industry.

ISBN: 978-1-962825-12-2

Powered By
C-SUITE NETWORK

THANK YOU!

FOR GETTING YOUR COPY OF

SECRETS OF TOP LUXURY AGENTS

You've made a great decision, and I'm so excited you invested in Secrets Of Top Luxury Agents! This book will help you change your business and challenges you and your team to do business differently and offer a better experience to your clients.

Hello there, I'm Michael LaFido, author of "Secrets Of Top Luxury Agents." As we crafted this book, our aim was to provide inspiration for newer or experienced agents that are looking to break into luxury while delivering valuable insights and practical but yet advanced strategies for seasoned luxury agents that are seeking a competitive edge in their market. Each author shares their unique journey, offering invaluable perspectives and experiences.

As you read through this book, take detailed notes, because it is jam packed with golden nuggets and secrets from 23 top luxury agents and 3 rising star agents. If you have doubts that you too can be a luxury agent, you are not alone! We specifically asked each of the co-authors several questions. You will see some questions are the same, some will be different for each chapter. However, there are 3 questions in each chapter we asked all the co-authors to answer. The first question asked in each chapter "Describe your first luxury sale, did you represent the buyer or seller, and how did the buyer or seller find out about you and vice versa?" Each author was also asked to give some recommendations for consumers, specifically, home sellers and home buyers. This bonus section can be found at the end of each chapter. Our goal is for you to eventually bring the same value described in the bonus sections to buyers and sellers. In doing so, you can leave copies of this book with potential clients on your initial appointment, and they will see YOU demonstrate the same qualities of the top luxury agents that are outlined in this book.

We invite you to join our Facebook community. Scan the QR code to join our community.

When you join, please take a picture of yourself holding up this book, and post that picture in our group introducing yourself to our group and your biggest "ah-ha" takeaway from this book. Use the hashtag #LuxuryListingSpecialist in the post.

Thanks again for investing in yourself with the purchase of this book. I can't wait to hear about your success story.

Prove Them Wrong,

Michael Lafido

SECRETS OF TOP LUXURY AGENTS

*Become The #1 Trusted Luxury Agent Today &
Dominate Your Market*

Michael LaFido

The real estate industry has been doing the same things over and over again when it comes to selling luxury homes. In most marketplaces today the same handful of agents are selling most of the luxury homes. The good news for you is the vast majority of agents rely solely on traditional marketing approaches taught by their brokers or real estate school. This practice personifies the definition of insanity: doing the same thing repeatedly and expecting different results.

If you commit to reading this book and take it very seriously, you will you be able to attract more high-end clients. More importantly you will become the trusted luxury agent to buyers, sellers, and referring sources. Buyers will cheerfully sign a Buyer Representation Agreement.

It's time to raise the standards and take matters into your own hands, the National Association Of Realtors (NAR) isn't going to save you. Together, let's elevate the industry standards and pave the way for unparalleled success. It's time to take control of your destiny in the world of luxury real estate. Let's prove them wrong!

For the *FREE* resources mentioned in this book, and to find out more about the Co-authors or coaching visit:
SecretsOfTopLuxuryAgents.com

Michael LaFido Founder & CEO

E: Michael@MarketingLuxuryGroup.com

"Michael's books and training are impactful; they give luxury agents the edge they need to elevate their business." **Chris Heller - Founder, President of OJO Labs and Movoto.com Former CEO, Keller Williams Realty International**

"This book is a roadmap to success in luxury real estate. Direct and invaluable." **Stefan Swanepoel - Executive Chairman T3 Sixty | New York Times Best-Selling Author**

"Strategies that cut to the chase and deliver. Outstanding resource." ***Tami*** **Bonnell - CEO, EXIT Realty Corp. International**

"This book should not just be in every Realtor's library, but it should sit on their DESK - easily accessible every day." **Michael Maher - Author, 7L: The Seven Levels Communication: Go From Relationships to Referrals**

"Straight talk, strong medicine, and actionable insights from the smartest professionals in luxury real estate. I highly recommend Michael LaFido's book to all established and aspiring luxury real estate agents and brokers." **Mickey ALAM KHAN - CEO, Luxury Roundtable, Former President, Luxury Portfolio International**

"You will learn proven techniques to better serve the higher-end market." **Amber Bonasoro - RE/MAX International Executive Director, Luxury**

"Michael LaFido offers a practical approach to educating REALTORS on how to be successful in the luxury market." **Rita K Blevins - Director of Professional Development, Houston Association of Realtors**

"Wow, I have never seen a more impressive approach to listing and marketing multi-million-dollar properties. If you want to break into the multi-million-dollar property market, or learn how to get your luxury listing sold, Michael is the person to talk to." **Judy LaDeur - Founder and President of The Profitable Recruiter and Judy LaDeur International**

"If you're ready to be more successful and reach a higher level, then read Mike's book. He has a true passion for making a positive difference!" James Malinchak - **Featured on ABC's Hit TV Show, Secret Millionaire Author of the Top-Selling Book, Millionaire Success Secrets, Founder, www.MillionaireFreeBook.com**

"As agents there are many courses and books to choose from, but not all of them have substance! Michael is in the trenches and practices what he preaches." **Olivier Mevellec - Co-founder & President of Global Marketing Agent**

"Michael LaFido has developed a blueprint for success that gives both Realtors and broker owners a turnkey system to dominate listing and selling luxury homes in ANY market." **Chad Roffers - Founder & CEO Concierge Auctions**

"If you want to market high-end properties, then Michael's Luxury books and his LUXE Designation is a must. He is the expert, and he leads by example with his impressive portfolio of $1 million + listings and sales." **Mark Wolfe - Owner of RE/MAX DFW Associates**

"Michael LaFido Changes the Real Estate Game with His Latest Book Anthology Secrets of Top Luxury Agents." **- Silicone Valley Times**

"Michael's most recent book, Secrets Of Top Luxury Agents, is a must-read how-to on achieving excellence as a luxury real estate professional. His practical approach and years of experience in the industry can guide any agent to success." **- Meghan Barry, President, Who's Who in Luxury Real Estate / LuxuryRealEstate.com**

ABOUT THE AUTHOR

Michael LaFido, the founder of the Marketing Luxury Group, assists other real estate agents, team leaders, brokers, by providing top-tier services including consulting and coaching. Michael has over twenty years of experience in the real estate industry. He is the author of the books "Luxury Listing Specialist", "Marketing Luxury" and founder of the Luxury Listing Specialist Designation (LUXE). This LUXE Designation establishes an in-depth and detailed set of standards for agents that represent luxury homes and is currently offered for Continuing Education (CE) in several states.

Michael and his company have been recognized and Michael has won many awards over the years. A partial list of those awards includes: Winning 'Best Property Consulting/Marketing' company by the International Property Awards. Michael was awarded MVP (Most Valued Partner) by "Who's Who in Luxury Real Estate" (www.LuxuryRealEstate.com). Michael was named " #1 Luxury Real Estate Coach in America" by fellow agents in Agent Magazine. Michael was just named a "Trailblazer" by RisMedia for his dedication to increasing diversity in luxury real estate.

Michael also has his own podcast, 'Luxury Listing Specialist". This podcast is on itunes and the other popular podcast platforms

Many agents within the industry are calling Michael's methods "The New Standard" for marketing luxury homes today.

Interested in getting Certified In Luxury?

Visit: LuxeDesignation.com for more information on the Luxury Listing Specialist Designation or scan the QR Code below.

DEDICATION

This book is dedicated to all agents, whether new to real estate or seasoned veterans, striving to elevate their average sales price and establish themselves as trusted luxury agents in their respective markets.

Many among us have grown disillusioned with the "traditional" methods of marketing luxury homes—or rather, the lack thereof. It's not your fault. The majority of agents have not received adequate training. This book exists to rectify that gap, aiming to empower agents while safeguarding consumer interests.

Perhaps you find yourself affiliated with a small boutique, a large firm, or a franchise. Most brokerages lack specialization in luxury real estate, relegating their luxury division to little more than a fancy logo and a fancy yard sign. You might have anticipated cutting-edge marketing support from your company, only to receive the same tired training and collateral as everyone else.

If this scenario resonates with you, then this book is your blueprint. It's time to seize control of your business. Your reputation and how others perceive your brand is at stake. This book will show you how to dominate luxury listings in your market by attracting the right clients and getting their homes sold. You will also learn best practices to bring more value to buyers so that they will cheerfully agree to sign buyers agency agreements and pay your fee for you to represent them.

For the FREE resources mentioned in this book, and to find out more about the Co-authors or coaching visit:

SecretsOfTopLuxuryAgents.com

LUXURY SPECIALIST DESIGNATION (LUXE)

24/7 ONLINE ACCESS TO ALL TRAINING AND MATERIALS

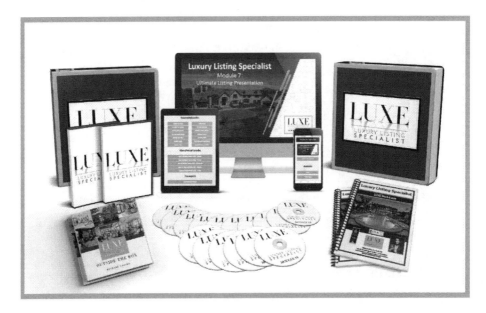

Interested in getting certified in luxury? LUXE requires zero previous luxury home sales to get certified in luxury. This course in taught both in person and on demand with a self-paced option through LUXE University. The LUXE Designation establishes a new set of standards for agents. Certified Luxury Agents with the LUXE Designation have been shattering records in their markets and have been increasing their average sales prices. Don't just take our word for it, take a look at all the reviews and case studies.

LUXE requires zero previous luxury sales to take this course and get certified in luxury. LUXE can be taken in person or via an online self-paced course and you have access to all materials online or you can take the class in person. With this Designation, agents have access to proven and repeatable marketing systems, which can be utilized in the marketing of their luxury listings.

To learn more on the LUXE Designation, please visit
LuxeDesignation.com

LUXURY LISTING
SPECIALIST PODCAST

LESSONS LEARNED: A LOOK BACK AT OUR MOST POPULAR EPISODES!

DOMINATE HIGH END LISTINGS IN ANY MARKET

HOSTED BY MICHAEL LAFIDO
LUXURY REAL ESTATE EXPERT, SPEAKER & TRAINER

EPISODE #300

Want to break into selling high end homes?
Subscribe to the Luxury Listing Specialist Podcast

LuxuryListingPodcast.com

Please leave us a 5 star review if you have learned something this book or from listening to our Podcast.

ReviewLuxeNow.com

GET INVOLVED WITH YOUR LOCAL DIVERSITY AFFINITY GROUPS

Grow your network, your referral base, and become an ally today!

AREAA - Asian Real Estate Association Of America
https://www.areaa.org/

NAREB - National Association Of Real Estate Brokers
https://www.nareb.com/

LGBTQ+ Real Estate Alliance
https://realestatealliance.org/

NAHREP - The National Association Of Hispanic Real Estate Professionals
https://nahrep.org/

FREE Resources & downloads!
Scan Below

Scan the QR Code For A FREE List Of The Companies We recommend For Website Development, Lead Generation, Prospecting, CRM's, & All Other Services To Help You Become The Leading Luxury Agent In Your Market

GET YOUR FIRST LUXURY LISTING WITHOUT SPENDING ANY MONEY ON MARKETING

Are you ready to break into the world of luxury real estate without breaking the bank?

- Expert Insights & Proven Strategies

- Maximize Success, Minimize Investment

- Immediate Impact With Actionable Steps

- How To Build Connections & Expand Your Network

*Get it **NOW** at*

LuxuryListingBlueprint.com

CONTENTS

> "
> You can't just look at price per square foot when pricing luxury homes – there are so many other factors involved.
> "
>
> Michael LaFido

GLENN STEARNS

From Underdog to Undercover Billionaire
Lessons Learned

G LENN STEARNS went from underdog to Undercover Billion-aire. He began with the decks stacked against him with alcoholic parents, failing the 4th grade, and fathering a child at age 14.

Through grit and determination, he rose to become an industry leader in the mortgage world, growing his namesake company to be the #1 mortgage lending company in the country.

He starred in the Discovery Channel's reality TV show Undercover Billionaire following his 90-day journey to anonymously build a $1 million company with $100 in his pocket, a pick-up truck, and a cellphone.

He launched his new legacy, Kind Lending, to revolutionize the mortgage industry. His memoir "InteGRITy - My Slow and Painful Journey to Success" is a Wall Street Journal Best Seller.

He is a proud father of six and husband to Mindy Stearns. Known for his philanthropy, Glenn is expanding to include mentorship through his and Mindy's podcast "Grit Happens."

Michael LaFido:

How can real estate agents apply principles from 'Undercover Billionaire' to enhance the development of their luxury real estate business?

Glenn Stearns:

When I built the business on "Undercover Billionaire," I was like any real estate agent or anyone else building their own business. What I did can transfer across just about any industry. There are a few guiding principles I have used my whole life to be successful in business. One of them is to never confuse effort with results. We work hard, trying to stay busy, but are we really getting the results we want?

Find your buyer first. A lot of times we go out fishing in the wrong pond. We need to make sure we're connecting with people who are willing to buy what we have.

Also, you can turn rivals into revenue. Sometimes we look at competitors and think they're the ones we must go up against every day, but it's also good to be friendly with your competition. You can end up working together. If you stay across the street and keep competing against each other, sure, it helps drive us. But if you get to know your competition well, you never know what opportunities come from that. Get close to your competition, they could end up being someone you can work with in the future.

Michael LaFido:

Given your substantial time spent in the LA area and California, coupled with extensive travel experience, it's likely you've acquired real estate. When evaluating agents for comfort, particularly in the pursuit of a secondary home in an unfamiliar area, what principles or qualities do you prioritize in selecting the agent you trust the most?

Glenn Stearns:

I've been fortunate enough to buy a few homes and properties in affluent areas, so I've experienced different styles of real estate agents. Twice, I've bought the most expensive property in a community, breaking the glass ceiling in the neighborhood. The most important aspect for me was could I trust the agent's ability to articulate my offer in a non-offensive way?

Agents just starting might think their job is to write up a contract, but that's the farthest thing from being a great agent. A great agent knows their community so well they can help present an offer that's not insulting to a seller. I want a great deal, so when I offer something lower than expected, the agent paints the picture for me. A great agent is an artist, putting together all the pieces, showing land value, reconstruction costs, and comps in the area. They support why my offer is fair. Maybe the seller doesn't like the number, but they understand how I got there. They craft the purchase and contract to give me the leverage I need, depending on the circumstances.

Michael LaFido:

What qualities do you look for as a home seller especially when interviewing an agent who's going to represent you and your family?

Glenn Stearns:

I've had agents who claimed they could secure a price I never dreamed of for my property, but it never materialized. What I learned was that professional agents, those who truly understood the market, could explain why a certain price was more likely to attract a buyer. As I've matured in terms of moving up into properties beyond a certain luxury level, having someone who truly understands the market makes a significant difference. They are incentivized to achieve the highest possible price while also getting the property sold.

You need to express your true motivation to an agent, and they, in turn, should provide advice on setting your listing price, estimating the time it may take, and assessing inventory and comparables. They do the same from the buyer's perspective, giving you solid advice. If an offer comes in, you're prepared, knowing, for instance, that homes at 10,000 square feet with ocean views are selling for $2,300 per square foot. This gives you a good sense of whether to accept an offer or wait it out. Especially in the higher-end market, where the market has been hot, having a great agent is crucial to help you navigate these decisions.

Michael LaFido:

Do you think being well-informed about all the comparables is essential, considering that some agents may tell sellers what they want to hear to secure a listing and later attribute price adjustments to market conditions or other factors, leading to frustration and a negative reputation for the entire profession?

Glenn Stearns:

Many individuals desire a sense of having made a good deal. Unfortunately, some agents, especially those in their early stages, might perceive their role as merely drafting contracts. In my opinion, this falls far short of what defines a great agent. A truly exceptional agent possesses an in-depth understanding of their community, enabling them to present offers that are not perceived as insulting by sellers. In my pursuit of a favorable deal, I ensure that when I propose an amount potentially lower than the seller's expectations, the agent skillfully paints the picture for me.

A great agent is akin to an artist, skillfully assembling various elements such as land value, reconstruction estimates, and comparable sales in the area. They can effectively articulate why my offer is fair. In such instances, the seller may not appreciate the offered amount, but they comprehend the rationale behind it. Furthermore, a skilled agent can draft the purchase and sale contract in a way that provides me with the necessary leverage based on the specific circumstances at hand.

Michael LaFido:

You brought up the word "trust." Let me ask you when you are determining which agent to represent you, is one of the questions you're asking yourself, "Can I trust this agent?"

Glenn Stearns:

There's this skeptical feeling that all they want to do is sell your property and make a commission. Then there are those who want you as a customer for life. They want to partner with you, so you've got to come across as a partner and be able to understand that sometimes it is emotional for a seller. You've got to support them in a way that they understand you're in it for the long run. I have an agent now in Orange County; I've worked with her for 23 years. We've gone through lots of great times, a few crashes, and a few things that didn't go so well. But this agent has been with me through every up and down, and she's been a wonderful, professional, supportive partner.

Michael LaFido:

What's one of your favorite books? Something you're reading now or one you would recommend.

Glenn Stearns:

Before delving into the book recommendation, I'd like to highlight an observation: the top two agents I know, one in New York and one in LA, both embody the authenticity you mentioned earlier. These women don't just lead in sales; they immerse themselves in their communities. Actively participating in charity events, cooking for families, engaging in 5K runs, they are more than just agents; they are invested community members. Their genuine care for their communities is a substantial factor in their remarkable success at the highest levels.

Now, onto the book recommendation. One that recently captivated me is "Chop Wood, Carry Water." It's a remarkable read that underscores the notion that success in life, business, or any endeavor isn't instantaneous. The book emphasizes the importance of time, patience, and starting with the fundamentals to foster growth, regardless of the speed at which we aspire to progress. Doing things correctly requires its own time, and to become a great agent, while you can engage in various activities and listen attentively, building your reputation in the community and earning trust is a gradual process. Much like the philosophy presented in "Chop Wood, Carry Water," taking the time to know people is crucial.

Michael LaFido:

In a culture obsessed with quick fixes, you stress the importance of patience and avoiding the search for shortcuts. Emphasizing the need to stick to the fundamentals, you've made it clear that success often requires time. Shifting gears to your book, "InteGRITy," could you provide a brief 30-second overview of its key themes?

Glenn Stearns:

Life is not a series of random events; it unfolds with purpose. Rather than happening to us, it happens for us. My book is a collection of personal stories, from becoming a parent at 14 and initially feeling overwhelmed to recognizing it as one of life's greatest gifts. Many experiences, initially unclear in their purpose, later revealed valuable lessons. I've come to appreciate that everything is part of my journey for a reason. In the end, I am deeply grateful and proud; I wouldn't alter a single detail.

Visit: SecretsOfTopLuxuryAgents.com
to learn more about Glenn Stearns

Connect with Glenn Stearns by Scanning the QR Code Below

PART 1

LUXURY SPECIALISTS

CHAPTER 1

MICHAEL LAFIDO

Innovative Marketing
Setting The New Standard In Luxury Real Estate

MICHAEL LAFIDO is a real estate consultant and top-producing Realtor with over twenty years of experience in the real estate industry and specializing in selling luxury homes that other agents failed at selling previously using aggressive and "outside the box" strategies and marketing

Michael's marketing has been the featured cover story in Crain's Chicago Business and highlighted in Forbes, Chicago Tribune, Mansion Global, Wall Street Journal and FOX News Chicago Business Hour to name a few. He is also the author of the books "Luxury Listing Specialist, "Outside The Box", and "Marketing Luxury".

Throughout his career, Michael learned the importance of high-caliber marketing versus "traditional marketing", which has become pivotal to his success. Over the past twenty years, LaFido and his team have developed a method that takes a more comprehensive, and proactive approach when positioning and marketing a home.

Michael, the founder of the Marketing Luxury Group, assists other real estate agents and affluent home-owners by providing top-tier services including consulting, lifestyle marketing, public relations and coaching to help agents and owners sell their luxury homes, utilizing his proven and repeatable strategies.

Michael has created the nationally recognized luxury designation for real estate agents which is known as Luxury Listing Specialist (LUXE). This Designation establishes an in-depth and detailed set of standards for agents that represent luxury homes and is currently offered for Continuing Education (CE) for real estate agents in many states. These trainings are based on the same principles Michael outlines in his book, "Luxury Listing Specialist" and he teaches to agents throughout the states and internationally.

Michael was awarded the MVP (Most Valued Partner) by "Who's Who in Luxury Real Estate" (www.LuxuryRealEstate.com), was recognized as a "Newsmaker" by RisMedia, and was voted "Top Luxury Real Estate Coach In America" by his peers in a major publication.

Many agents within the industry are calling Michael's methods "The New Standard" for marketing luxury homes today.

Initially, I hadn't planned on contributing a chapter in this book about my own journey. However, many of my co-authors and peers insisted that I include my insights in this compilation. So, here I am, Michael LaFido, hailing from Chicagoland, ready to share my story to you.

The first question we posed to others, and one I'll now answer:

Would you share the story of your first luxury sale? Were you representing the buyer or the seller in this transaction?

Michael LaFido:

It was a truly memorable sale, representing the seller of a remarkable property. They reached out after receiving one of our canceled and expired mailing letters, a strategy I used extensively. Despite their tardiness to our meeting (he showed up 3 hours late), my enthusiasm for the opportunity kept him engaged. Armed with our video book, we presented a bold plan to position their home aggressively in the market.

During our discussion, the seller questioned why I hadn't shown interest in his property earlier, given it was previously listed for sale with two other agents. I candidly explained that if he sought a conventional local agent, I wasn't the right fit. However, if he desired an unconventional, proactive approach with a proven marketing strategy and a vast database, then I was the ideal choice.

While I hadn't yet closed a major multimillion-dollar sale at that time, he liked my enthusiasm and creativity and took a leap of faith, granting me the chance to prove myself. For that opportunity, I remain grateful. That listing opened up so many more relationships and opportunities for my business.

How do you stay current with market trends and changes in the luxury real estate industry, and how do you apply this knowledge to benefit your clients?

Michael LaFido:

Over the past 5 years I have attended, on average, over 10 real estate events per year. We have a huge network of both top agents, team leaders, top brokers, and strategic businesses that cater to the best in the real estate industry. To use a sports example, don't go where the soccer ball is....go where it is going. Think ahead. I'm able to know first hand about market trends and future trends by attending these events. I get to find out what is working currently and what is on the horizon. For example, with the recent big lawsuit against brokerages and NAR regarding buyers agents commissions being paid by sellers...10 months prior to this being headline news...I already was planning for this outcome because I attended the invite only T3 Summit and heard from some experts on the pending lawsuit. By attending these events I also get to find out what tech companies and what marketing strategies are working in other markets. I am a big believer that "Best marketer beats best agent", so if I can bring a marketing strategy back to my team...we have a competitive advantage.

How do you work with other professionals in the industry, such as architects, designers, and attorneys, to provide comprehensive services to your clients?

Michael LaFido:

I have been a big believer the easiest way to "get in" with high net worth individuals is to bring value to their circle of trust and their service providers they already trust and are doing business with. I understand these other business owners and professionals' time and energy is important, so I don't waste it. I realized early in my career their most listened to radio station in their head is WIIFM, "What's In It For Me". For the most part they primarily care about themselves, and making more money so what can I do to bring value to them and help their business grow and be more profitable... directly through referrals and indirectly through introductions and "what's working today" marketing suggestions. If I am consistent and bring value then I will be "top of mind awareness" when they hear of someone thinking of buying or selling a home...and hopefully refer them to me or make an introduction. I believe the best way to get a referral is GIVE a referral.

If you had to identify one factor that distinguishes yourself from other luxury agents in your local market, what would it be? Additionally, what guidance would you offer to those aspiring to walk a similar path?

Michael LaFido:

Firstly, my philosophy revolves around the notion that "It's not the market, it's the marketing". What truly sets me apart is my approach to marketing properties. We don't simply list them on the MLS and hope for the best. Instead, we are proactive and meticulously scrutinize each property from a discerning perspective.

Imagine yourself as a skeptical buyer considering multiple properties. Why should you choose this one over others? We adopt this buyer-centric viewpoint and strive to present everything on a silver platter, from curb appeal to staging, ensuring that every aspect of the home is showcased effectively. In today's fast-paced digital age, where first impressions are everything, our photos and videos need to be not just good, but outstanding. We understand the importance of showcasing the right features and creating a compelling narrative through visuals.

Another crucial aspect of our approach is video marketing. We collaborate with talented videographers to create cinematic masterpieces that showcase properties in the best possible light. From stunning aerial shots captured by drones to carefully choreographed scenes featuring actors and even horses, our videos are designed to captivate and engage prospective buyers.

We've gone to great lengths to produce compelling video content, shooting footage from helicopters, planes, trains, and automobiles. Our dedication to innovation paid off when we became the pioneers of lifestyle videos in the Chicagoland market. This groundbreaking initiative caught the attention of Crain's Chicago Business, a publication revered by affluent readers akin to the Wall Street Journal. They featured our $10,000 video, which showcased the property with horses and Lamborghinis, further solidifying our reputation as trailblazers in luxury real estate marketing. The owner was quoted as saying "Michael's marketing is the "new age" of real estate marketing."

One of the most memorable transactions in our portfolio was the sale of what we fondly refer to as the "taxidermist home" in River Forest, just outside Chicago. This property presented a unique challenge due to its unconventional decor, including over a hundred taxidermy animals. Despite the odds, we seized the opportunity and embarked on a transformative journey to market the property effectively.

This sale not only showcased our ability to overcome obstacles but also highlighted our commitment to delivering exceptional results for our clients.

Each property we encounter presents a unique opportunity for us to craft a bespoke marketing plan tailored to its individual characteristics. Our willingness to embrace challenges and think outside the box has earned us a reputation for attracting and successfully marketing difficult and unique properties.

In essence, our commitment to innovative marketing strategies and our dedication to showcasing a property's "best features" in the best possible light set us apart in the luxury real estate market.

How do I approach prospecting for luxury clients and what strategies have been most successful?

Michael LaFido:

The most successful strategy for us has been growing our network. We firmly believe in the adage that the best way to receive a referral is by giving one first. Engaging with Chamber of Commerce events, networking groups, nonprofit organizations, and charity outings has allowed us to expand our network significantly. Building genuine relationships, being memorable, and establishing trust are paramount. People prefer doing business with those they like and trust, even if it means paying a higher price for a superior product or service. For us, luxury isn't just about a price point; it's about delivering exceptional customer service and creating an unforgettable experience, akin to the renowned Ritz-Carlton standard. Our approach to prospecting high-net-worth individuals involves being personable, avoiding pushiness, and focusing on persistent follow-ups.

To stay abreast of market trends and changes in luxury real estate, we remain plugged into various webinars, forums, and conferences. Understanding the interests, hobbies, and evolving preferences of high-net-worth individuals is crucial. What's in vogue today may not be tomorrow, so we prioritize staying ahead of the curve. Collaborating with interior designers, architects, stagers, builders, and legal professionals enables us to offer comprehensive services tailored to our clients' needs.

Working with other industry professionals involves careful vetting and selection. We believe that our referrals reflect on us, so we only partner with those who share our commitment to excellence, integrity, and fairness. It's crucial that our partners deliver on their promises, exceed expectations, and provide value to our clients. By nurturing these relationships and consistently adding value, we create a mutually beneficial ecosystem where referrals flow naturally, ultimately benefiting all parties involved.

How do I describe my process for pricing luxury homes?

Michael LaFido:

Determining the value of unique and luxury properties is far from a cookie-cutter process. We adopt a comprehensive approach that begins with assessing the land's worth. Understanding the value of the property itself involves factoring in its age, considering depreciation, and analyzing comparable sales data—even if it means looking well beyond the immediate area where data might be scarce.

Our record sales in areas with limited comps are often met with questions from buyers and their agents about our pricing methodology. In response, we provide detailed explanations, often referring them to expert appraisers for further clarification.

Beyond these basics, we also rely on intuition honed by market analysis. We assess factors like timing, location, quality, finishes, and overall appeal for potential buyers. Pricing isn't solely based on square footage; instead, we consider what we call "profit activators," which encompass a range of variables contributing to the property's value. We also determine if there is a gap in the market with limited inventory in this price point or is there a backlog of inventory sitting at this price point.

Understanding that what someone has invested in a property doesn't dictate its market worth is crucial. Location plays a significant role, as does the prevailing market conditions—be it a seller's, buyer's, or balanced/neutral market.

Ultimately, determining the price of luxury properties requires a nuanced understanding of various factors. And as with any investment, market value is what buyers are willing to pay, irrespective of past investments. This analogy holds true whether it's about real estate or stocks like Apple—value is determined by market demand, not by personal investment.

I hope this sheds some light on our pricing strategies.

What's my marketing strategy for luxury homes? And it's a specialized approach. What channels do I use to reach high net worth buyers and sellers?

Michael LaFido:

My approach to marketing luxury properties is highly tailored and personalized. While there are foundational elements like stunning photos that accentuate the property's best features and downplay any less favorable aspects, I delve deeper to understand the target audience, their preferences, and interests. Factors like local or out-of-area buyers, lifestyle preferences, importance of schools, and proximity to amenities are all considered. Luxury isn't just about brick and mortar; it's about selling a lifestyle, safety, and evoking emotion and experience. I aim to create marketing materials that allow potential buyers to envision themselves living in the property. For instance, one of my early lifestyle videos was aptly titled "Imagine."

My marketing strategy encompasses various channels, including print, digital, word of mouth, and proactive outreach. I believe in being adaptive and responsive, adjusting strategies based on feedback and conducting SWOT analyses to identify strengths, weaknesses, opportunities, and threats in the market. This analysis helps inform not only the marketing approach but also pricing strategies.

To reach high-net-worth individuals, I leverage a vast database of potential buyers and sellers, some of whom may be open to off-market transactions for the right price. Additionally, I'm affiliated with organizations that cater to affluent clientele, and I employ a mix of direct mail, handwritten correspondence, digital marketing, and word-of-mouth tactics. When necessary, I'm not averse to more unconventional methods like door-to-door visits—I believe in doing whatever it takes to stand out from the competition. Now, let's move on to the bonus questions tailored to consumers.

Bonus Section

Tips for Home Sellers

These next questions are geared towards the consumer. It's for a homeowner that's interviewing Realtors to sell their high end and/ or unique home. What should they look for in determining which agent is best to market their home?

Michael LaFido:

First, it's crucial to assess their track record in selling homes similar to yours. What is their network like? Experience speaks volumes, but if they lack a track record, look for hunger and creativity. Communication is key—are you going to be in direct contact with them or someone from their team? Recently, a seller chose to work with me over the top agent in Illinois because they wanted direct access to me. They knew with the other agent they would not be dealing with her...they'd be dealing with a team member.

Inquiring about their marketing plan and proven track record is essential. Do they have a database of potential buyers? Can they redirect disappointed buyers from similar listed properties to the subject property? Trust is paramount. Transparency and honesty build trust. Like a good doctor, an agent should provide honest assessments and solutions, even if that information is not what the seller wants to hear.

Potential sellers should research the agent online, to ensure the agent's online presence reflects results, expertise and integrity. Knowledge about not just local markets but also property features and finishes is crucial. Ultimately, sellers need an agent who can sell their home for top dollar, provide honest guidance, navigate challenges, and have a team to support them through the process.

Tips for Home Buyers

The next tip is for somebody buying a home either in their local market or maybe it's a vacation property. What qualities should a buyer look for in an agent to help them decide if they should hire that agent and sign A Buyer Representation Agreement with them?

Michael LaFido:

In today's market, inventory is scarce, making it crucial to partner with an agent who is proactive, well-connected, and insightful. Look for someone who acts as an advisor, not just a salesperson, guiding a buyer toward wise investments rather than quick sales. A comprehensive approach is key, along with access to off-market properties—those hidden gems not available to the public.

A trustworthy agent with a vast network and access to off-market listings is essential. They should serve as a matchmaker, connecting you with properties that align with your needs and preferences. Trust and network size are paramount considerations in choosing the right buyer's agent.

Visit: SecretsOfTopLuxuryAgents.com
to learn more about Michael LaFido
Connect with Michael LaFido by Scanning the QR Code Below

CHAPTER 2

JACK COTTON

Selling Luxury with Integrity
The Cornerstone of a Real Estate Icon

WORDS OF WISDOM from a Real Estate icon with 50 years in the industry. Growing up on Cape Cod, Jack found that the supply of scrap lumber from home construction was perfect for building forts and tree houses. "I would retreat to one of my crudely built homes, either in the woods or up in the trees, and all would become right in my world," Cotton remembers. "I call that the treehouse feeling." In 2005,he purchased a custom treehouse from one of the premier builders in California and arranged for it to be brought across the country, along with a tree trunk. "I have it set up in my front yard," he shares. "It reminds me daily of what drives me in this business and why it is so important to help other people achieve that treehouse feeling."

Jack specializes in waterfront estates and village properties. In the business for 50 years, he is known for his integrity and discretion, coupled with a low-key and consultative style. "The question I ask myself many times a day is, 'What is in the best interest of my client?' "I believe that is the cornerstone of my success."

"Most people in the real estate business are in it as a means to an end," he observes. "For me, it is the means and the end."

A spouse, father, and grandfather, Jack is an avid cyclist. He also loves boating and can be found exploring the nooks and crannies of Nantucket Sound and neighboring islands throughout the summer.

Michael LaFido:

Think back to your first luxury sale. Did you represent the buyer or the seller and how did you get the opportunity to work with them?

Jack Cotton:

My inaugural luxury sale occurred in the early 1970s, involving a property that fetched $96,000 at the time—considered a significant sum back then. Remarkably, I represented both the buyer and the seller in this transaction.

When advising aspiring luxury real estate professionals, I often stress the importance of identifying the Maverick in their market— the individual willing to take a chance on someone new, audacious, and unproven. Mavericks typically stand out by residing in multimillion-dollar homes while driving unconventional vehicles. My first luxury sale epitomizes this advice, as a Maverick played a pivotal role in giving me that initial opportunity. Starting my real estate company at the age of 21, I was determined to establish myself as an expert, delving into markets, value, and pricing through rigorous appraisal classes.

Beyond traditional real estate transactions, I expanded my expertise by conducting valuation analyses to assist clients in lowering property taxes and for estate planning purposes. Notably, my early business focus centered on working with widows. Having grown up without grandparents but with a deep connection to older individuals, I adopted a protective and caring role toward these widows, providing guidance and counsel as if they were my own family. This unique approach, coupled with my valuation proficiency, fueled the growth of my business.

During an era when women often weren't primary decision-makers in financial matters, I encountered a widow whose husband, a partner in a prominent law firm, had passed away. Fed up with being directed by her late husband's partners, she sought independence and took a chance on me. Representing both her and the buyer of her house, this deal led to another opportunity—an adjacent property that the second generation couldn't afford to keep. Facilitating the sale to the next-door neighbor, I successfully completed my first luxury transaction, further cementing my journey into the world of high-end real estate.

Michael LaFido:

What distinguishes you from other agents in the luxury market?

Jack Cotton:

Honestly, Michael, there are individuals in my market who outshine me in marketing and socializing. They excel in everything. However, I stand out when it comes to answering a question, I repeatedly ask myself throughout the day, maybe once an hour or every half hour one question: "What is in the best interest of the client?"

Most people, when the chips are down, cannot put the client first. But I can and I do.

For instance, when my company grew, I had agents who would come to me with a moral dilemma. Every time, I would ask, "What's in the best interest of the client?" At that point they instantly knew what the right thing to do was.

Michael LaFido:

What guidance would you offer to fellow agents seeking to differentiate themselves in their local market?

Jack Cotton:

Absolutely, establishing expertise is paramount.

In my small town of 4,500 residents, surprisingly, we have around 23 billionaires. Given their busy schedules, personal interactions are limited, making reputation crucial. Becoming an expert in your market and understanding the nuances of value is foundational.

Once mastery in these areas is achieved, the next step is pricing expertise. What is your approach to pricing, and how do you articulate it convincingly?

Market preparation is equally vital. Being adept at getting properties ready for sale is a key differentiator in capturing high-net-worth clients.

Marketing prowess is a significant factor. How do you strategically showcase properties to the world? What's your approach to making these properties stand out?

Lastly, negotiation expertise is paramount. When dealing with individuals involved in transactions worth hundreds of millions or even billions of dollars, being perceived as an expert negotiator becomes crucial. Despite my background growing up on the "wrong side of the tracks," I've navigated this world, and the key to leveling the playing field has been establishing myself as an expert, particularly in negotiation. How do you approach leveling the playing field in your dealings with high-profile clients?

Michael LaFido:

What is your approach to sourcing luxury clients, and which strategies have proven most effective for expanding your network?

Jack Cotton:

Honestly, divine guidance led me toward specializing in expertise and becoming proficient in markets, value, and pricing.

Building my business revolved around taking market and value data and applying it to individual properties, a crucial approach for clientele fixated on their net worth and minimizing taxes. Particularly, property taxes and inheritance taxes are intensely disliked.

Notably, expensive properties are often held by trusts or LLCs to mitigate estate taxes. Placing a property in a trust necessitates an annual up-to-date valuation, crucial for the trust to become fully vested to beneficiaries eventually. The property owner then rents it back from the trust, a process scrutinized by the IRS. To address this, I conduct a rental analysis to determine the fair rental value.

Conducting these valuation analyses has not only built my business but also set me apart from competitors, leveling the playing field with more experienced agents. How have you approached differentiation in your real estate business, and what strategies have you found effective?

Michael LaFido:

Could you share details about a complex transaction you've navigated in the luxury real estate space, particularly within the upper price range?

Jack Cotton:

This spring, I handled the sale of my neighbor's impressive house, but it turned out to be one of the most challenging transactions I've experienced.

Adding to the complexity of this $11m transaction, the buyers committed to purchasing the property without physically viewing it. Whether it was the stakes involved at this price point or protecting a buyer in a sight-unseen transaction, the advisors involved seemed more interested in finding problems than solving them.

In contrast, our approach is not centered on performance or trying to impress. Instead, we concentrate on addressing challenges and collaborating with all parties involved. We don't actively seek problems; our goal is to solve them and foster collaboration.

Michael LaFido:

How can you effectively handle a client's expectations to ensure they feel well-informed, satisfied, and inclined to leave you a five-star review upon conclusion?

Jack Cotton:

Tell people what they should expect from us, and then we do more. It's as simple as that. Also, have systems in place for everything you do.

Michael LaFido:

What is your approach to marketing homes, and how do you tailor your strategy to reach high-net-worth individuals in a way that sets you apart from others in the industry?

Jack Cotton:

Here's my perspective on this. In my experience, most high-net-worth individuals in the real estate market already have some connection to the area. While there are instances where people enter a market without prior ties, often, about nine out of ten have a pre-existing connection.

My strategy revolves around robust marketing targeted at the existing community. However, the key lies in the approach to this kind of marketing. We prioritize storytelling, aiming to unearth and convey a compelling narrative for each property. The goal is to create a story that resonates with buyers, prompting them to eagerly share it with friends once they become homeowners.

I strongly believe that agents should be prominently featured in property videos. Being a part of the narrative allows agents to convey the story effectively and connect with potential buyers on a more personal level.

Bonus Section

Tips for Home Sellers

Michael LaFido:

The following questions are directed towards homeowners. What advice would you offer to someone with a unique or distinctive property? How should they assess and choose a listing agent to effectively market and represent their high-end or unique property?

Jack Cotton:

I can provide an answer that addresses both buyers and sellers.

Preparation is paramount. Whether you are a seller or a buyer, it's crucial to be prepared for that initial appointment. We extend the same advice to agents. As a consumer meeting with an agent, take the time to prepare your questions in advance. What information do you want to glean from the agent? Create a list of questions, covering aspects such as their pricing process, marketing strategies, advertising philosophy, unique selling propositions, approach to showcasing properties, and how they qualify potential buyers. Being well-prepared ensures a more productive and informed discussion.

Tips for Home Buyers

Michael LaFido:

What additional advice would you offer to someone in search of a property, whether it's in their primary residence or a secondary destination like a lake house or ski resort? What qualities should a buyer look for in an agent to help them decide if they should hire that agent and sign A Buyer Representation Agreement with them?

Jack Cotton:

Certainly, my experience in the marketplace has provided me with valuable insights into various property types, including lake and oceanfront homes. I have a solid understanding of conservation rules, ensuring that properties adhere to environmental regulations.

In terms of off-market properties, I employ diverse strategies to discover exclusive listings, and I typically find a notable number through these efforts. My process involves promptly communicating these opportunities to clients, ensuring they are informed about unique and exclusive options.

As for the homebuying process, you will directly work with me throughout the journey. I believe in providing personalized attention and guidance to ensure a smooth and tailored experience. This is a fundamental aspect that both buyers and sellers prioritize, and I am committed to delivering a high level of service.

Visit: SecretsOfTopLuxuryAgents.com
to learn more about Jack Cotton

Connect with Jack Cotton by Scanning the QR Code Below

CHAPTER 3

FRANK AAZAMI

Cultivating Excellence in Client Service and Satisfaction

FRANK AAZAMI along with his Private Client Group global advisory team deliver a lifelong entrepreneurship experience as added value for their client base. As a successful small business owner, media (Top 40 Radio) promoter, real estate investor, and developer; he can manage your next real estate move. Frank's success has been proven through his high level of commitment and ability to utilize creative financing options such as seller carries, wraparound mortgage transactions, Trades, 1031 Exchanges, lease/purchase contracts and tailored agreements for sales: protecting clients' best interests.

His level of commitment is solely focused on uniting buyers and sellers; emerging win-win closings and along the way exceeding clients' expectations. Managing clients' entire real estate portfolios is his niche; his interview process identifies clients' objectives to effectively deliver positive results through traditional and creative contracts. Before custom-tailoring a constructive marketing plan; he maps out the best possible approach to gain traction and epic results. His white glove "concierge service" has earned Private Client Group a reputation for excellence. As an inspired member of the National Association of Realtors and a proud member of Russ Lyon | Sotheby's International Realty; the Private Client Group has earned many endorsements both locally and internationally.

Frank's Global Team represents properties within 83 countries, territories, and locally here in Paradise Valley, Scottsdale (including North Scottsdale, Silverleaf, DC Ranch, Estancia, Desert Highlands, Desert Mountain, Troon, Greyhawk), Phoenix (including Biltmore Estates, Arcadia), Fountain Hills, Carefree, Cave Creek plus other 2nd and 3rd homeownership destinations through his Sotheby's International Realty affiliates.

Michael LaFido:

On your first luxury sale did you represent the buyer, or the seller? How did they find out about you, and vice versa?

Frank Aazami:

I entered the marketplace during a challenging period, witnessing a downturn with properties going under short sell, selling for less, and facing foreclosures. My perspective was geared towards making a difference by saving one family at a time. The primary motivation behind my entry into the market was to prevent families from losing their homes. To achieve this, I organized gatherings and brought agents together to brainstorm innovative approaches to selling properties, avoiding the one-size-fits-all mentality.

My commitment to helping families and reshaping the way properties were sold led to a movement. In collaboration with agents, we worked on strategies not commonly taught in real estate school. Recognizing the importance of finances, I started receiving referrals from agents, establishing myself in the marketplace after moving from the East Coast to Arizona two decades ago.

My wife often questioned how I managed to secure listings and why clients were choosing me. I explained that while I offered to co-list, many preferred to give it to me as a referral. I accepted these assignments, ensuring that I genuinely connected with the families and could provide valuable assistance.

During the real estate challenges, I felt like I was throwing lifelines one at a time, akin to the Titanic sinking. A notable instance involved an investor with multiple properties, one of which had lingered on the market despite being listed by top agents in the area.

Taking on the assignment, I strategized on how to sell a luxury listing that others doubted. I invited tours, handled skepticism from fellow agents, and eventually sold it myself. The property found its new owner in a high-profile musical performer set to perform at the Super Bowl halftime, though I'll refrain from disclosing the name.

Throughout the process, I represented both sides and encountered challenges, such as being pressured by someone claiming to know the performer's manager. I stood my ground, asserting that they weren't the procuring cause, and successfully navigated the situation, ultimately leaving both parties satisfied with the transaction.

Michael LaFido:

If you were to pick one thing that sets you apart from other agents in your local market when it comes to luxury real estate, what would that be, and what advice would you have for agents?

Frank Aazami:

Let's talk about the two types of representation. There are agents who simply take orders, they're essentially order-takers. You tell them what you want, and they nod along, like a magic mirror telling you that you're the fairest of them all.

On the other hand, there's the advisor approach, and that's the role I aim to embody. Often, clients don't initially hire me; it might take a second or third round before they do. However, our track record of getting properties sold spans two decades. I've often asked clients why they didn't hire me the first time we met.

Some would say, "I just didn't think you needed it." Maybe it was because I rolled up in a nice car or always showed up in a tie, projecting a professional image befitting the luxury real estate market. I strive to maintain a high level of professionalism because that's what bankers and advisors do – they dress up for the occasion.

Others might say, "You didn't think you could sell it for that." I'd counter, "Well, was I right or wrong? You didn't sell it, and here you are, talking to me years later."

When I assess a property, I base it on market value, understanding the pulse of the market, its trends, and the values from street to street, style to style, size, and level of finishes. We consider all aspects and then make recommendations.

Michael, just like everything else we purchase in life, whether it's toothpaste or a toothbrush, we buy by comparison. Real estate is no different. Buyers are making decisions based on competitive positioning, and it's crucial to either assist someone in selling or compete and win that sale against others.

Michael LaFido:

A lot of these high-net-worth individuals are used to people catering to their schedule, to their time. They're busybodies. But for you, as an agent, how do you still provide personalized attention to your clients, as well as manage other clients, run a business and still have personal time for yourself? You're not a one-stop shop. You don't have one or two listings. You have multiple buyers and sellers. The question is, how do you provide both personalized attention to your clients, while still managing the multiple high-value buyers and sellers at once?

Frank Aazami:

First and foremost, I don't entertain calls that are filled with baloney. If the conversation veers away from what needs attention, I keep it brief. This ensures that I can focus on quality calls that require servicing during both business and non-business hours. If you're calling just to chat, chat, chat, that's not my style. I'll politely inform you that I have another call coming, which is usually the case.

Managing time efficiently is crucial. It's important for clients to recognize that I am a professional advisor, not their friend. While I'm open to listening, it's essential to reach out about matters I can genuinely assist with. For instance, don't call me about your mover; I'll guide you to the best mover. Similarly, plumbing issues should prompt a call to a plumber, not me. I serve as a resource, directing people to the right professionals.

Collaboration is key, and I work with a team. Contrary to those who claim to pay for clients' movers, that's not my approach. I avoid getting involved in such things because I prioritize understanding clients' true needs before making any commitments.

Having recently experienced moving after several years in the same home, I realized how heavy and challenging it can be. This personal experience has heightened my empathy for others going through the same process. To streamline tasks, I bring in a team of assistants who handle various aspects of my projects. From paperwork to marketing and scheduling, each assistant plays a crucial role. While I'm capable of doing it all myself, having a team elevates the level of service provided. If someone were to leave the team, I wouldn't be left stranded, as I know how to handle every aspect of the job.

Michael LaFido:

What is your process for pricing a unique property, a luxury home, when there's no true comparable? A lot of these are bespoke, custom. They are not cookie cutter by any means. Please describe your process in pricing these homes.

Frank Aazami:

I evaluate properties based on quality – both in terms of materials used and workmanship. Of course, the age-old mantra "location, location, location" remains a top priority. It's crucial to consider what the market can bear, especially when a significant investment, like building a $30 million home, is at stake. The question becomes, can the market support such a value, and is the homeowner prepared for potential challenges, such as selling or needing to sell in the future?

When working with individuals in the design and building phase, my approach is to establish a connection early on. I emphasize the importance of a sellable floor plan and acceptable interior finishes, offering advice upfront to avoid unpleasant surprises later. Being a good advisor involves not only protecting clients' financial interests but also guiding them towards improvements.

There are those who make purchases based on personal desires – a want-buy. Whether it's a Luxury handbag or a Bentley, these items may not be necessities, but individuals buy them because they want them. In such cases, my role may not involve advising against such choices, but rather facilitating the process for those who are determined to fulfill their desires.

However, there are instances where we serve clients who may have made decisions a decade ago, and we need to have candid conversations about the current market value of their property. It's essential to convey that potential buyers must either love the place, the price, or something about it for a successful sale. Setting a realistic timeframe is also crucial, and I make it clear that success requires either time or price flexibility. I won't sign up for a scenario where there's no love for the place, price or the client I will be servicing.

Reflecting on my experiences, I acknowledge a mistake made before the pandemic, underestimating the trading potential of certain homes. The market dynamics unexpectedly shifted, causing a surge in demand, and properties that I had doubts about ended up selling rapidly. It serves as a reminder that favorable market conditions are not constant and must be assessed carefully.

Michael LaFido:

Are you saying that if they're not realistic on price or not considering an aggressive short-term pricing strategy, you are not interested in taking an overpriced listing for a brief period?

Frank Aazami:

Certainly, under certain terms, I'm not interested. I tend to think outside the box, you know? If I'm negotiating on your behalf, I'm also negotiating for myself. So, in this scenario, you could cut a check for $100,000 designated for marketing, and I'd commit to working for you for the next 90 days. That sum would cover all my expenses, and I'd essentially work for you at a rate of $100,000.

Now, here's the unique twist – if we successfully sell the property, that $100,000 becomes part of the compensation adjustment. Think of it like a draw. When you work for a developer, there might not be immediate sales because of various tasks like infrastructure development, home construction, community preparation, and obtaining the Certificate of Occupancy. In such cases, they implement a draw contract.

Michael LaFido:

How do you go about differentiating and adding value so that your communication is clear? Your customer support and service are commendable, and you consistently deliver on your promises. Can you elaborate on the specific actions you take to bring value to your referral sources, such as lenders, title companies, and possibly attorneys? I recall you mentioning offline that you recently received a referral from someone in Carmel-by-the-Sea, California.

Could you share insights into how you differentiate both within and outside the Sotheby's brand? In an industry where everyone knows a real estate agent, how do you maintain your value and stand out?

Frank Aazami:

Attend these gatherings organized by different brands, whether they're national or international. I started attending when I was just getting started, and I made it a point to attend every single one of them. We've crossed paths multiple times at these events. Regardless of whether your brand directly hosts such gatherings, if they are associated with luxury real estate or any other niche, make sure to participate.

Brands like RE/MAX, Sotheby's, and Coldwell Banker all organize these events. Attend, familiarize yourself with your peers and team members nationwide and globally. Identify the best individuals—those with the right character, demeanor, intentions, and commitment to service—and integrate them into your team. Build an international team, engage in regular communication, send updates, and schedule annual in-person meetings.

Both of us engage in teaching and improving others' skills, a more challenging task than merely attending an event. It's about being a host rather than just showing up at the party. This approach is what fosters connections and generates referrals. Remember, handing out referrals never results in financial loss; it's a profit-making strategy. Some companies even base their entire revenue on referrals, though not all opportunities may be genuine. Personally, I prefer referrals from people I know rather than unsolicited calls from unknown sources.

Michael LaFido:

Let's move on to technology. It's a big buzzword today. Right? Last year, I went to NAR's conference, technology, whether it be blockchain a couple of years ago, to ChatGPT.

What technology and tools do you utilize to support your work as an agent, as a luxury real estate agent? And what do you do to ensure that you stay ahead of the curve?

Frank Aazami:

I personally explore all available tools, but I prioritize those that are user-friendly. I've encountered many tools where I subscribed for a year but found them challenging to use, resulting in non-utilization. However, I encourage experimentation—touch, feel, and play with various tools. It's akin to buying a game; if you don't like it, you won't return it—it just expires or fades away. There's no harm in trying different tools; it's about finding what works best for you. What will make the phone ring? What aids in better organization, tracking, and assembling a comprehensive CMA presentation, market analysis, or lead capturing?

I make it a point to test every tool available, whether it's through Sotheby's or other platforms. We have a backend with a plethora of technologies and apps, and I specifically seek out those that haven't been widely tried before. I rely on the fact that they've been qualified and recommended by others. Instead of randomly googling and risking the use of untrustworthy tools, I prefer going with something that someone has vetted and recommended as a reliable brand.

Michael LaFido:

When you secure a significant or distinctive property, could you share insights into your marketing strategy for such homes? How do you set yourself apart locally or nationally with a specialized approach? Additionally, what channels do you employ to connect with high-net-worth individuals, potential buyers, or influential figures who may be aware of someone seeking to purchase in that area?

Frank Aazami:

In terms of marketing, I believe in going back to the beginning, essentially ground zero. I delve into the history of the property, exploring the initial vision when there was no structure. Why did the owner choose this site? Who were the key individuals involved, from architects to designers and builders? What was the inspiration behind the design? Every property, every address, has a unique story waiting to be uncovered. We explore the details of the property, from the choice of renowned brands like Sub-Zero to the materials used, such as granite and plank floors.

I emphasize the narrative of how the property was assembled, making it more memorable. For each home, I enlist the expertise of a writer or journalist to interview various people associated with the property, be it the designer, architect, homeowner, or builder. This approach breathes new life into dated properties, examining what improvements can be made.

Leveraging technology, I incorporate AI into the marketing strategy. For instance, in a community project centered around car enthusiasts, I used AI to generate renderings of dream garages. By illustrating different options, such as higher or lower ceilings, underground spaces, skylights, and lifts, we aim to capture the imagination of potential buyers. These renderings go beyond static images, with some even presented as videos, creating a more immersive experience for prospective clients. The goal is to spark excitement and motivation by showcasing the possibilities and potential of the property.

Bonus Section

Tips for Home Sellers

Michael LaFido:

Now, we're going to make the transition to benefits for the consumer in the chapter. During this section we're talking about tips for sellers, tips for buyers.

My first question to you would be, for someone that owns a home that they're thinking about selling, what's the number one tip or two or three tips and suggestions you'd have for a homeowner that's interviewing agents or a single agent? What should they look for when hiring an agent to represent them, whether it be their primary residence or a vacation property? What do you recommend to that homeowner?

Frank Aazami:

Over the past several years, my role has evolved to encompass the management of my client's entire portfolio, extending beyond a single property in the current marketplace.

To break it down, I conduct interviews with agents in various markets and subsequently provide my recommendation. It's truly astonishing to witness the claims some agents make about being number one when, as someone deeply entrenched in the industry, I can discern the actual volume of their transactions. Through thorough interviews, I pose the right questions, delving into their strategies, the value they bring, and the concrete actions they plan to take. I inquire about their plans for the first and second weeks, their contingency measures if initial efforts fall short, and their overall approach to garnering attention, generating interest, securing contracts, and navigating the entire process.

When I conduct interviews, my focus is on understanding what the individual agent brings to the table, not just what the company claims to offer. While there may be a list of advertising placements on paper, the key question for me is whether we will genuinely be included, and will the agent take responsibility for our presence in those placements?

I embarked on obtaining my license because of past experiences where promises were made but not fulfilled. I was told that certain actions would be taken on my behalf, but when I inquired, the response was often a vague reassurance like, "It's coming. Just hold on." After three or four months of waiting, with no visible results, I decided to take matters into my own hands.

An audit by the IRS a few years ago reinforced the importance of substantiating claims with tangible evidence. The audit focused on understanding why I invested a significant amount of money in marketing. Upon completion, and after presenting the proof of my efforts, the IRS acknowledged the substantial effort I put into marketing my listings and even recommended my approach to others.

My advice is simple: If you commit to doing something, follow through and demonstrate it to me. I emphasize this because, as part of my client engagement strategy, I regularly send them updates showcasing something unique we did for them—whether it's in print, on social media, or through digital means. For digital efforts, I provide metrics like the number of eyeballs and clicks, which clients appreciate.

Retention is about transparency and delivering results. When it comes to negotiating extended contracts, I am straightforward with clients, asking if they want to adjust the pricing or continue with the current strategy. The feedback I often receive is that my approach is a refreshing change compared to their previous experiences with agents who didn't deliver on their promises.

Tips for Home Buyers

Michael LaFido:

For someone buying a home, things might be a little bit different. What should sellers consider when hiring an agent. What advice would you have for the buyer, as to which agent they should consider representing them when they're purchasing? What qualities should a buyer look for in an agent to help them decide if they should hire that agent and sign A Buyer Representation Agreement with them?

Frank Aazami:

Hire a local expert – someone familiar with every street and property, someone with extensive experience in selling and listing within that area. Choose someone well-versed in the specific market you aim to enter, as many transactions occur before properties officially hit the market. Consider the "coming soon" concept – a strategy I recently employed by securing a property with an escalation clause in a competitive market. We strategically utilized our network, particularly our sphere, to navigate this pre-listing phase.

The buyer's broker, being from the area, understood the value and acted as our advocate. Recognizing the competitiveness of the situation, he insisted on an escalation clause, aligning with our pricing strategy. This emphasizes the importance of hiring someone who comprehensively knows the market.

Professionals not only understand the properties but also the community and neighbors. Utilizing your sphere and existing clients, you can broadcast specific buyer needs. This approach often leads to fruitful interactions, such as a neighbor mentioning a potential match while putting out the trash. These types of transactions underscore the significance of relationships and a profound understanding of the market.

Visit: SecretsOfTopLuxuryAgents.com
to learn more about Frank Aazami

Connect with Frank Aazami by Scanning the QR Code Below

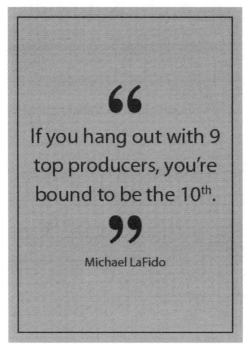

CHAPTER 4

JULIE FAUPEL

Cultivating a Global Network for Local Real Estate Success

JULIE FAUPEL is a top-producing real estate professional, the Founder and CEO of REALM, the most elite membership of real estate professionals ever assembled. REALM involvement is invitation only and includes a patented technology platform that enriches individual client data while activating the databases of the membership in a completely anonymized manner.

Prior to her real estate success, Julie worked for 12 years in management and consulting for luxury hotels and small businesses. Julie has served on the Jackson Hole Community Foundation Board and is the former Jackson Hole Chamber of Commerce Board Chair. Julie served on the Christie's International Real Estate Global Advisory Board and is a member of the Young Presidents Organization.

Julie and her husband are avid supporters of entrepreneurship as trustees of the Silicon Couloir and independent investors in several start-up ventures. Julie loves to entertain and bring people together. Julie and Matt are both graduates of the Hoffman Institute, and they host an annual reunion for Hoffman Graduates at their home in Jackson Hole.

Michael LaFido:

Tell me about your inaugural luxury real estate transaction. Were you acting on behalf of the buyer or the seller, and what led to initial connection?

Julie Faupel:

During an open house in a stunning ski chalet at the foot of a mountain resort, a family residing in a neighboring high-value mountain ski home walked in. Expressing interest in purchasing any properties going into foreclosure over the next 20 months (pre-recession, pre-2008), I initially doubted the likelihood in Jackson Hole. However, as foreclosures unfolded, I reached out to them, and we engaged in opportunistic transactions—perhaps not at the $9 million or $10 million level as during the open house, but still totaling millions of dollars over time.

Reflecting on this experience, I've gleaned two valuable lessons: first, the importance of building a personal network, and second, the realization that luxury is a mindset. Guiding them through foreclosure transactions, short sales, and assisting in portfolio building forged a strong relationship. Over the years, we've completed numerous transactions, ranging from basic condos to downtown office buildings and multi-million-dollar deals.

My initial transaction, where I represented the seller during the open house but later worked with the buyers, marked my introduction to working with luxury clients.

Michael LaFido:

How do you leverage your knowledge of market trends in luxury real estate to educate your buyers, sellers, and prospects?

Julie Faupel:

In resort destinations like Jackson Hole, where I operate, staying current with the market trends is essential. We are primarily a second-home market, and our fortunes are often linked to the conditions of the buyers' primary markets. To stay informed, we closely monitor urban markets like New York City, San Francisco, and Los Angeles, as well as regional factors from cities like Atlanta, Dallas, and Houston.

International factors also play a role. Understanding what drives these markets and influences buyer psychology is crucial. Furthermore, we keep an eye on changing aesthetic preferences in architecture and home features, as this impacts property values and demand in our area. For instance, the recent shift towards open spaces and indoor-outdoor living became vital due to lifestyle changes during the pandemic. We can better serve our clients by staying informed and adapting to evolving preferences. We should also make sure we counsel our sellers who are considering doing home renovations. It's important that we pay attention to what the preferences are going to be because that helps impact value and demand long term.

Michael LaFido:

Navigating shifting preferences and comprehending regional dynamics is crucial in the luxury market. Which skills and qualities have proven most valuable in your career, and how have you cultivated them over time?

Julie Faupel:

Success in luxury real estate hinges on several crucial qualities and skills. Foremost among them is resilience. Penetrating the luxury market demands persistent effort, as success is more tied to mindset than initial achievements. Dressing for the role you aspire to holds significance, along with cultivating the right mindset and taking appropriate actions.

I've consistently viewed luxury real estate as a partnership, approaching each transaction with a mindset that ensures I remain a trusted advisor to my clients. It's essential to maintain a holistic perspective, considering the community and the desired lifestyle throughout the process.

At times, frank conversations with sellers become necessary, especially when a property isn't selling or the market is resistant to the price point or style of the home. Engaging in these candid discussions and being honest is crucial. Expressing sentiments like, "We're both partners in the success of this transaction," fosters a positive mindset, helps keep emotions in check, and ensures focus on the desired outcome.

Michael LaFido:

In a fiercely competitive market like Jackson Hole, how do you set yourself and your brand apart, and what strategies do you employ to sustain a robust reputation and referral network within the community?

Julie Faupel:

My husband and I both are joiners. We volunteer a lot. In fact, my husband, Matt, was the one who said, "If we expect this community to make us successful, we need to make sure that we're making this community successful."

I think that kind of mentality of showing up, giving back and being there for the community has added to our reputation. In a competitive market like Jackson Hole, building a strong reputation and referral network is crucial. People notice your behavior and the positive impact you make, whether through philanthropy, board involvement, or other activities. These connections often lead to referrals and strengthen your network. In addition to community involvement, we've also focused on industry engagement. Giving back to the real estate industry and challenging peers to elevate their performance has expanded our referral network significantly. Currently, about 80% of our business comes from referrals.

Michael LaFido:

What technology and tools do you utilize to support your work as a luxury agent, and how do you stay ahead of the curve in terms of innovation?

Julie Faupel:

Technology plays a crucial role in luxury real estate, and staying ahead of the curve is essential. Leveraging data and information from the internet, AI, and other technological advancements is crucial. Platforms, like REALM which I developed, help us access and analyze data on markets, clients, lifestyles, and migration patterns. This information enhances our advice and decision-making for clients. However, it's important not to replace human expertise with technology but to use it to augment our abilities. Luxury real estate remains a personal transaction, and the more data and technology can inform our advice, the better we can help clients make educated decisions about their desired lifestyle and property choices.

Michael LaFido:

Which specific characteristics or abilities do you possess that have proven particularly advantageous in your luxury real estate career?

Julie Faupel:

I describe myself as a "people collector," finding joy in cultivating relationships with a diverse range of individuals. My network reflects this eclectic group, spanning various backgrounds. This ability to connect people and build friendships has been a cornerstone of my career, extending beyond property transactions to assist clients in seamlessly integrating into the community. I see my role as more than just selling homes; it involves introducing clients to their initial circle of friends, guiding them toward philanthropic opportunities, assisting with school choices, and connecting them with outdoor activities. This holistic approach not only enhances their lives but also results in increased referrals and transactions. Building relationships and fostering a sense of community has been a secret ingredient that has proven successful for me.

Looking ahead, the future of luxury real estate, especially in resort markets like Jackson Hole, is promising. The pandemic has amplified the demand for remote work and open spaces, aligning perfectly with our offerings. Buyers aren't just in search of properties; they seek a lifestyle, and the resort market caters to this aspiration. However, with advancing technology, increased competition is inevitable. Agents must embrace technological tools such as AI and predictive analytics while remaining grounded in real estate fundamentals and relationship-building. Monitoring demographic shifts is crucial, as the preferences of younger buyers will shape the market in the years ahead. My advice to aspiring agents in this field is to be patient, prioritize relationship-building, and commit to continuous education. Recognize that luxury is more about mindset than merely a price point. By staying dedicated to your clients' success and expanding your sphere of influence, success will naturally follow.

Bonus Section

Tips for Home Sellers

Michael LaFido:

What is the number one recommendation you have for a home-owner who owns a high-end property regarding the qualities they should look for in a Realtor to sell their home?

Julie Faupel:

This goes back to style. I have always sold on enthusiasm. It makes me sad when someone says this broker came over and told me all the bad things about my home. Why would you do that to someone? You want someone who represents your house who is proud to be there, excited to be there, and excited to be part of that business transaction.

It's not sheer unabashed enthusiasm, It is enthusiasm with a business mind.How are they coming at this as a partner and how are they going to optimize that sale for you. It's the combination of the two. It's important to have balance but it's important to have both those assets.

Tips for Buyers

Michael LaFido:

What is your number one suggestion for luxury buyers interviewing agents? What qualities should a buyer look for in an agent to help them decide if they should hire that agent and sign A Buyer Representation Agreement with them?

Julie Faupel:

It goes back to being a great listener and community involvement piece. How well do they know this place and how involved are they overall in the community. It helps on a number of fronts, not just helping them get to know the community but also what awareness they are going to have about latent inventory, pocket listing or inventory getting ready to go on the market. A lot of times having that advantage or that insight from your broker is the thing that gets them the dream home they are looking for. We had clients who had a cookout at their house and we were laughing because it never hit the market, and it didn't even appraise it ended up being the most successful deals of the decade. It was because we had the inside track and they trusted that we would. When it came down to it they bought it sight unseen. We are talking about a multi-million dollar listing. We were going through the house filming it on our iphone. It's all those things market knowledge, insight and how connected they are within the community.

Visit: SecretsOfTopLuxuryAgents.com
to learn more about Julie Faupel

Connect with Julie Faupel by Scanning the QR Code Below

CHAPTER 5

RICHARD SILVER

The Art of Privacy and Discretion in High-Profile Transactions

RICHARD SILVER, a renowned Sales Representative and the dynamic leader of Silver Burtnick & Associates at Sotheby's International Realty Canada, is a paragon of excellence in luxury real estate. With prestigious designations such as ABR, e-PRO, and Certified International Property Specialist (CIPS), Richard brings unparalleled expertise and dedication to his clients, ensuring an exceptional real estate experience that surpasses expectations.

His journey in real estate is marked by significant achievements and leadership roles. As a past Director-at-Large for the Canadian Real Estate Association and former President of the Toronto Regional Real Estate Board, Richard's deep understanding of the market dynamics and extensive knowledge make him a sought-after authority in the industry.

Beyond his impressive real estate credentials, Richard is a recognized technology and real estate voice. His insights on the impact of international markets on the industry and his prowess as a speaker and writer position him at the forefront of the digital transformation in real estate. His tenure as the founding President of the Asian Real Estate Association of America's Toronto Chapter and as a founding member of REALM-Global, an exclusive network of elite luxury real estate professionals, further cements his status as an influential figure in the sector.

Inman News acknowledged Richard's significant contributions by naming him one of the "Top 100 Most Influential People in Real Estate for 2013," a testament to his far-reaching impact. His role as an Inman Connect Luxury Ambassador further exemplifies his commitment to excellence in luxury real estate.

Fluent in French and steadily expanding his linguistic repertoire with Spanish, Richard's multicultural approach enhances his ability to cater to a diverse clientele. His foresight in recognizing the critical role of the Internet and digital marketing in real estate has been pivotal. He has seamlessly integrated cutting-edge technologies into his team's strategies, benefiting buyers and sellers with innovative solutions and unparalleled market insights.

Richard Silver's distinguished career is a testament to his real estate mastery and a reflection of his unwavering commitment to elevating the standard of service and excellence in the luxury real estate market.

Michael LaFido:

Talk to us about your first luxury sale and how did find you and vice versa? Did you represent the buyer or the seller?

Richard Silver:

I've always tried to maintain strong relationships with fellow agents. In one instance, an agent sought me out due to my specialization in the Heritage District, known for its vast collection of Victorian homes. The property in question was a Victorian mini-mansion, and the agent wanted me to guide her client through the sale, eventually resulting in a successful purchase.

However, a few years later, the client decided to sell the property as it didn't align with her retirement plans. This client was high-profile, leading to substantial media interest. Despite the property's uniqueness, I chose to remain discreet about the buyer's identity, keeping information close to my chest. While I was open to discussing details about the house, I prioritized safeguarding the client's privacy.

Unfortunately, another agent from a different office breached this confidentiality by sharing the floor plans with a national media outlet, posing a security risk for the individuals involved. Regardless of whether there's a Non-Disclosure Agreement (NDA) in place, I strongly believe in safeguarding information and respecting people's privacy. The media, driven by its agenda to obtain stories, tends to amplify both positive and negative narratives, particularly when it involves individuals of high net worth.

Michael LaFido:

If you were to pick one thing that sets you apart from other agents in the Toronto market or just in the industry in general, what would that be and what advice would you have for agents in regards to that differentiator?

Richard Silver:

I've always been an advocate for embracing new technologies, whether it's AI, the internet, or social media. Instead of shying away, I believe in exploring how these tools can be leveraged to our advantage, serving as time-savers and efficiency enhancers. Networking has been a cornerstone of my approach, attending numerous events, both local and international, to establish connections.

Being able to assure clients that I can cater to their needs, whether they are moving to a secondary property, looking to find or sell one, is crucial. I've cultivated global connections that allow me to introduce clients to the best opportunities worldwide. As members of Realm Global, you and I both understand the value of this network. Additionally, my affiliation with Sotheby's, renowned for its cachet, has proven beneficial, garnering referrals even from the auction arm.

Networking, maintaining a stellar reputation, and consistently going the extra mile are key components of my strategy. Rather than just considering actions like calling someone or taking them out for dinner, I actively take those steps to be present and exceed expectations.

Michael LaFido:

How do you approach prospecting for luxury clients and what strategies have been most successful in you building your network of high net worth individuals?

Richard Silver:

I have a longstanding presence in the industry, and I've observed that my clientele has matured over the years. Many of them, whom I initially met as they were entering or establishing their businesses, have progressed through various property transactions, moving from lower to higher-priced areas. I've consistently stayed connected with them through these transitions.

My client base now extends to include their children and, in a few instances, even their grandchildren. The key to this enduring relationship is unwavering consistency. I make it a priority to always be available for my clients, serving as a reliable source of information. While I don't provide direct legal advice, I position myself as the "source of the source." In other words, I assist in connecting clients with professionals, such as lawyers for specialized needs, ensuring they receive the best guidance without offering legal advice myself.

Michael LaFido:

Talk about managing client's expectations to ensure they feel fully informed and satisfied with the services you provide. Also, do you have any suggestions on how you are able to manage expectations?

Richard Silver:

Staying abreast of market dynamics is crucial. This involves keeping a keen eye on sales, legislative changes, and emerging trends. For instance, when a new mansion tax was introduced in Toronto, I proactively advised certain buyers to expedite their property purchases before the year-end to mitigate increased tax implications post-January 1st. This foresight led to significant transactions in the final months of the year.

Remaining informed about available properties, understanding buyers' preferences, and providing timely advice contribute to a successful partnership. Regular communication ensures I grasp their evolving needs. Additionally, I leverage AI and other tools to provide monthly updates on the Toronto, Canadian, and US real estate markets, positioning myself as a reliable source of information. While the ultimate decision rests with the clients, I aim to empower them with the insights needed to make informed choices.

Michael LaFido:

There might be some overlap in this question, but how do you differentiate yourself? Toronto, it's not a lower price point market, right? There's a lot of luxury competition when it comes to other real estate agents. How do you maintain your strong reputation, your referral network, and again, differentiate yourself? Anything you want to add to that?

Richard Silver:

I attend various events and conferences to add value for my clients. Whether it's an international marketing event to network with agents worldwide or attending Sotheby's conferences as the GTA representative for the interior marketing team, I stay connected to the global real estate community. Toronto has long been a hub for international buyers, making my involvement with Sotheby's valuable.

Being part of Sotheby's allows me to assist other agents seeking referrals, serving as the go-to person for finding the best agents in different locations. This role aligns with my commitment to being a reliable source of information, ensuring my clients have access to the top-notch services they deserve.

Michael LaFido:

Talk to me about technology. You mentioned AI briefly, but what technology and tools do you utilize to support your work as a luxury real estate agent, and how do you ensure you're staying ahead of the curve in this evolving market?

Richard Silver:

First of all, I go to a lot of conferences where there is information about technology. And there's also, rather than hiding my head under the blanket, I just force myself to find out as much as I can about the new technology and how to use it. And I use technology, yes, to become more efficient. But I also try and use it as a time saver. I can now, with the new advances in AI, I can take a press release from the Toronto Real Estate Board and I can convert it into visual presentation, a PowerPoint presentation, in probably under one minute. And then I post that to all my clients. It becomes part of my newsletter. And I have a very substantial newsletter list, both for clients and also, for agents around the world so that they know what's happening in Toronto and that hopefully, I'm the person that they connect with if they have somebody they need to refer to the Toronto marketplace.

Michael LaFido:

Let's move on to individual pricing for properties, right? We have readership that are newer agents. We have seasoned veterans who are reading the book and pricing unique properties. I'd love to hear your process, your system for doing that when there's no true comparable to use. Can you describe your process for pricing a luxury property?

Richard Silver:

I follow a two-step process when determining a property's price. Firstly, I conduct a thorough examination of the property, assessing the competition, recent sales, and current listings. In the high-end market, where pricing can be challenging, understanding the dynamics of selling or not selling is crucial. Additionally, I utilize Automated Valuation Modules (AVMs) to track the property's value increase over time.

Considering the changes in the market and any enhancements made to the property, I gather information on the work done. Considering their initial purchase price, market fluctuations, and the value added to the property, I formulate a price estimate. Ultimately, reaching an agreement between the seller's expectations and the market reality is vital. Communicating potential listing prices, emphasizing a range, and aiming for the top end while being prepared to consider lower prices contribute to a successful strategy. Despite the challenges in the real estate market, establishing a realistic price range ensures adaptability to market conditions.

Michael LaFido:

How often do you revisit price? Do you do it based on, obviously if there's new listings, new sales. Do you tell them, "Hey, we're going to test the market for 30 days, 60 days, 90 days?" How do you have that conversation ahead of time so that when you do have that conversation when it's listed, they're prepared for it, I guess?

Richard Silver:

I thoroughly discuss our property marketing strategies, keeping clients consistently informed about online views and the number of showings. Monitoring the showing frequency serves as a valuable barometer; a slowdown could indicate an issue. It's essential to interpret the data correctly – consistent showings without offers may suggest curiosity rather than genuine interest.

Gaining feedback from agents who show the property helps uncover potential obstacles preventing offers. Maintaining communication with other agents about their showings and promptly responding to inquiries is crucial. Every property showing generates valuable insights, and sharing client feedback with the listing agent is a practice I prioritize.

Understanding the opportunity cost of a property not selling is crucial. If a property remains vacant for an extended period, there are associated costs. Evaluating whether reallocating funds could yield better returns becomes important. Addressing the reluctance to accept lower offers or reduce the price is a personalized discussion. Sellers must provide informed and genuine responses, considering their motivation for selling the property.

Michael LaFido:

Talk to me about a marketing strategy. These homes require more love sometimes, as you know, and a specialized approach. What channels do you use to reach high net worth buyers and sellers, and talk to me a little bit about your marketing strategies?

Richard Silver:

Working with Sotheby's, I prioritize international property marketing, recognizing the value of reaching a global audience. Utilizing high-definition photos, video walkthroughs, and various video formats, I aim to craft a narrative for each property. Encouraging sellers and their children to share personal paragraphs about their favorite aspects of the house adds a unique touch to feature sheets, giving the property character and a familial connection.

Injecting personality into property descriptions helps potential buyers envision themselves in the home. Creating relatable content is crucial, and I often write it myself. Additionally, I leverage Chat GPT to refine the verbiage, ensuring a sophisticated tone.

Chat GPT acts as a valuable assistant, tailoring content to my personal voice and preferences. The paid version offers even more customization options, allowing me to save time and focus on client interactions.

Efficiency is a priority for me, and leveraging technology like Chat GPT enhances my ability to connect with clients and provide a personalized touch to property marketing.

Bonus Section

Tips for Home Sellers

Michael LaFido:

The first question is geared towards homeowners, whether it be their primary residence or their second, a vacation property. When interviewing agents to market their home, can you give a tip or two as to what they should look for when hiring an agent to best market their property and represent them on the sale of their property?

Richard Silver:

It's crucial to assess an agent's sphere of influence when choosing one to represent your property. While some agents might excel individually, a vast and diverse sphere of influence is essential for ensuring maximum visibility and connections for your property. This extends to international connections through brand affiliations, participation in events across various regions, and active engagement in different markets like Canada, the United States, and Europe.

Personally, I prioritize expanding my reach by connecting with offices during holidays, presenting market insights, and fostering collaboration. I believe an agent's influence should not be limited to the local scene but should span internationally for optimal exposure.

When selecting an agent, inquire about their recent sales and request access to contact their past clients. Seeking feedback directly from previous clients provides valuable insights into an agent's performance. Moreover, encouraging clients to share their experiences through Google reviews facilitates transparency and aids potential clients in making informed decisions.

In the digital age, online reputation matters. Regularly checking and contributing to Google reviews ensures an up-to-date reflection of an agent's credibility and professionalism. By simplifying the process for clients to leave reviews, you contribute to building trust and transparency in the real estate community.

Tips for Home Buyers

What qualities should a buyer look for in an agent to help them decide if they should hire that agent and sign A Buyer Representation Agreement with them?

Richard Silver:

I consider trust to be of utmost importance in real estate, as it forms the foundation of a successful client-agent relationship. In addition to trust, having comprehensive knowledge about the market is crucial, especially when dealing with specific property types like heritage properties or condominiums. Understanding the nuances of condominium laws, which differ significantly from freehold home laws, is essential. Whether clients are buying in Canada, the United States, or internationally, such as in Mexico or Europe, being well-versed in the legal aspects of property acquisition is indispensable.

For instance, in Mexico, properties within a certain proximity to the shore require purchase through a bank trust. Clarifying the implications of such legalities for buyers is a key responsibility. Recognizing the differences in laws, government regulations, and financing options is vital. In Mexico, securing financing is a lengthier process, and guiding clients through these transitions is a significant aspect of my role.

Many of my clients are at a stage where they are transitioning, often termed as "right-sizing." This may involve not only downsizing but also purchasing larger properties with specific features like single-floor layouts or condominium settings. Providing valuable advice and assistance during these transitions is a crucial part of my business. Clients rely on me to either possess the necessary knowledge or facilitate their access to pertinent information, enabling them to make informed decisions. As their guide, I prioritize keeping them well-informed throughout the decision-making process.

Visit: SecretsOfTopLuxuryAgents.com
to learn more about Richard Silver

Connect with Richard Silver by Scanning the QR Code Below

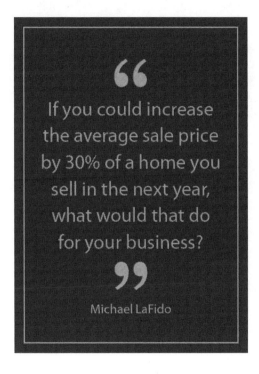

> " If you could increase the average sale price by 30% of a home you sell in the next year, what would that do for your business? "
>
> Michael LaFido

CHAPTER 6

TERRY SPRAGUE

Mastering Luxury Real Estate with Innovative Marketing

I am the owner and founder of LUXE | Forbes Global Properties, and the exclusive Oregon agent for Sport Star Relocation. I am consistently ranked as one of the top 10 brokers in the state of Oregon for sold listings and closed transactions representing buyers of high-end properties. Our office consistently ranks as one of the top brokerages in the state for closing high-end luxury properties. We are a true boutique, full-service real estate company serving clients from around the world. We specialize in delivering a concierge-based experience complemented by the highest definition of real estate advice, local knowledge, and unsurpassed regional and global marketing. Our brokers specialize in multiple disciplines including luxury properties, vineyards, equestrian, agricultural, coastal, special architecture, and specific locations within Oregon. Each situation and property are as unique as the individuals we represent. We take the time to discover how we can best serve the one-of-a-kind needs of every client, relying on our extensive resources and experience to provide a distinct level of expertise.

Michael LaFido:

Talk to us about your first luxury transaction. Did you represent the buyer side or the sales side? And how did they find out about you or how did you meet them?

Terry Sprague:

Early on, I recognized a key differentiator when I committed to the real estate business – I crafted a comprehensive business plan. This was back in '07, and my aim was clear: focus exclusively on properties valued at a million dollars or more. To immediately position myself among the desired inventory and clientele, I sought permission to conduct open houses for these high-end properties.

One notable instance was an Open House at a $2 million newly constructed, fully staged property. Little did I know that I would cross paths with NBA player LaMarcus Aldridge, who not only toured the property but also ended up submitting an offer, resulting in a $2.2 million transaction within my first week.

What seemed like a normal progression in the moment turned out to be exceptional. Everything fell into place as per the plan I had meticulously laid out. The next pivotal moment came when the builder of that luxury property, surprised that such houses were open to the public, approached me. Despite reservations from another broker who mentioned, "We don't normally hold open these types of houses," I seized the opportunity.

I not only held the open house but also sought permission to advertise the listing extensively. I invested in newspaper space, sent out postcards to potential buyers, and had brochures made. As a result, even in my first week, I visually represented luxury properties.

During this open house, the builder observed my interactions and materials. We engaged in a conversation about the economy, given the challenging times of 2007-2009. Impressed by the experience, the builder later proposed collaborating on an office space. While not an exclusive arrangement, it provided me with invaluable exposure and learning opportunities alongside a luxury home builder.

Two significant outcomes emerged from this period – I established a standard for the price point I operated in, achieved success, and forged a connection with the NBA. Additionally, meeting and collaborating with a luxury builder became a source of continuous learning over the ensuing years.

Michael LaFido:

If you were to pick one thing that sets you apart from other agents in your local market, everybody knows a real estate agent in your market and most markets, what would that be? That's number one and then what advice would you have for other agents to set themselves apart?

Terry Sprague:

So probably my strength is my weakness. I've never scaled. So a lot of very successful brokers in my space end up creating teams and leveraging and delegating, and I tend to take on less listings, but I tend to manage those listings when it comes to all the showings. And I don't know, I just think there's a certain magic that occurs when I meet a seller and they tell me the home story and they tell me the provenance and the history of why they bought it, why they built it, all the unique things they did.

And then I don't own a lockbox. I don't use Showing Time. I don't use artificial intelligence. Every showing, the broker must call me, and that includes outside third-party vendors that tend to text you. I ask them to call me. I want to see proof of funds. I want to know a little bit about the buyer. I want to be sure that they've reviewed all the documentation, the floor plan, that maybe they've even done a drive by, and that if we're doing a showing it's going to be agent to company, I'm going to be there, and the idea is you're coming with the intent of writing an offer.

Michael LaFido:

How do you manage expectations of the consumer, of your client, the seller in this case, or buyer, so that they feel fully informed on the level of services that you're offering as well as the market?

Terry Sprague:

Initially, there's the introduction, and sometimes, I find it necessary to provide a disclosure about my operating style. I recall an instance where I interviewed for a listing, but they chose two other brokers. Later, they reached out to me and expressed surprise, mentioning that they didn't think I liked their $2.5 million property. I apologized, explaining that my approach is somewhat surgical. When I enter a house, my focus isn't solely on praising its beauty to secure the listing. Instead, I immerse myself in the showing experience, anticipating potential objections.

To avoid coming across as critical, I make it a point to inform people in advance about my operating style. It's akin to visiting a doctor with a tumor and expecting practical discussions rather than compliments on appearance. Many clients in my specific marketplace appreciate the idea of someone managing their privacy, time, and preparation. I handle these aspects for them, ensuring that showings are a valuable use of their time. Whether I'm personally conducting the showing or shadowing from a distance to provide quality feedback, I am committed to managing the process effectively.

Michael LaFido:

How do you differentiate yourself in a highly competitive luxury real estate market, and how do you maintain a strong reputation and referral network?

Terry Sprague:

When I entered the real estate business, I brought a diverse set of formal backgrounds that enriched my approach. A significant aspect was my experience in merchandising retail, where I served as a clothing buyer for high-end Italian men's clothing. This background instilled in me the importance of presenting properties in a compelling way, akin to how merchandise is showcased.

Additionally, I had a financial background, having worked at Shearson Lehman Hutton in the '80s for 15 years. Following this, I had a transformative experience, akin to a "Jeremy McGuire moment," where I retired to the Caribbean in 2000. During the next six years, I delved into art, owning an art gallery and a restaurant, gaining diverse personal and professional experiences.

My entry into real estate was prompted by a house purchase upon returning to the United States due to family circumstances. Curiosity led me to write a business plan, keeping in mind the evolving landscape of real estate marketing. This was a time when online distribution and videos were emerging, and I constantly challenged myself on how to be a market leader.

Reflecting on my time at Christie's, exposure to a groundbreaking Australian company called Goldeneye inspired me. Investing $15,000 in a video with cutting-edge features, including one of the first professionally shot drone sequences, proved groundbreaking in '08-'09. This video, played at a Christie's owner's meeting in Paris, earned me the Christie's of the Year award globally.

While I may not be the largest producer in my market, I strive to be a thought market leader. The focus remains on selling visually appealing properties, capturing attention, telling compelling stories, and ensuring an impactful in-person presentation. Constantly challenging myself, I ask, "What could I do to disrupt myself and stand out in the market?"

Michael LaFido:

What are some strategies for identifying potential clients, luxury sellers, luxury buyers, and how do you market to them?

Terry Sprague:

I used to carry a Wayne Gretzky card in my wallet for about 15 years. When I moved to the Caribbean and went swimming with my wallet, it eventually dissolved. The Wayne Gretzky card had a quote that stuck with me: "While everyone focuses on where the puck is, I'm going to focus on where the puck is going to be." I believe business is that simple. Many talk about what they want to do but may not take the time to consider where the business is heading and how to position themselves accordingly.

Moving into a high-end residential area when purchasing our first house positioned me in a high-net-worth environment. One of the best pieces of advice I received was to put out 12 to 15 open house signs. Conducting open houses every Sunday, I challenged the conventional time frame, opting for a longer duration from 12:00 to 5:00. Rain or shine in Oregon, setting up those signs became a marathon, but it paid off.

Early in my career, people perceived me as having many listings because of the numerous signs. This strategy attracted high-net-worth individuals to high-net-worth houses, akin to planting a garden of tulip bulbs. While some Sundays had fewer interactions, there were multiple instances of selling houses at open houses. In my first nine months, I achieved $9 million in sales, and in the second year, I reached $26 million.

Building the optics of what I do and interacting with people effectively at open houses contributed to this success. Creating a welcoming space, I use a large neighborhood map on a dinner table as a conversation starter. Instead of bombarding visitors with questions, I often ask if they'd like to see a plat map and a floor plan before exploring the house.

This approach provides valuable information without coming across as sales-focused. I guide visitors to emotional spaces in the house, sharing floor plans and plat maps. Using a large map strategically, I engage visitors by asking if they know where they are on the map. This opens up conversations about their journey, making them comfortable without invading their space bubbles.

Even today, if I conduct an open house, people may approach me and express interest after going out to the car, reinforcing the effectiveness of this strategy.

Michael LaFido:

How do you manage expectations and communication with high-net-worth individuals?

Talk to us a little bit on managing expectations, mainly from a communication standpoint as well as you as an agent, multiple balls in the air with buyers, and sellers. How do you do it?

Terry Sprague:

I believe the secret sauce is simple: treat people the way you'd want to be treated. Just like when you enter a restaurant or a retail space, you appreciate someone turning their head to observe and recognize you. People desire recognition, observation, and effective communication.

It's noteworthy that you mentioned the Ritz-Carlton. I currently have the Ritz-Carlton development as one of my listings—a substantial $700 million project. Aligning with our mission plan, our business approach centers on people. Surround yourself with great people, establish a duplicable process, and aim to surprise and delight. While I borrowed these principles from different sources, combining them into people, process, surprise, and delight has proven effective.

The surprise and delight aspect involves providing concierge-level service and creating emotional connections. Leaving an imprint on people is crucial. We strive to emotionally connect with individuals, making them remember their experience with us. Despite investing in various unique marketing strategies, most of our business comes from word of mouth—people sharing their positive experiences.

Our team comprises two women—one handling contracts, and the other focused on market implementation. We invest considerable effort in preparing listings for the market, involving various third-party professionals like videographers, photographers, writers, appraisers, and contractors. While these individuals don't directly work for me, they have embraced the people, process, surprise, and delight philosophy. Clients often express that every person associated with our team is deeply committed to what we do, carrying the enthusiasm for delivering exceptional service.

Michael LaFido:

Describe your process for pricing a luxury property when you represent the seller?

Terry Sprague:

It's a thought-provoking question. When I initially entered the real estate business, I spotted a For Sale by Owner sign while driving around. I approached them, expressing interest in seeing the house, and eventually, they chose to list the property with me. My key inquiry was, "If I could sell it for as much as you intend to net by selling it on your own, could I represent you?" I listed the property, and when questioned by office brokers about my chosen comparable, I confidently asserted, "This will be the new comp," setting a slightly higher price, and successfully sold it at that rate.

Being actively engaged in the market daily, showing properties, gauging consumer responses to price points, and representing buyers while exploring properties, I've developed my own pricing algorithm. Although I leverage algorithm-based tools to analyze pricing, a significant portion relies on intuition. In the current market, I monitor it daily and assess potential listing prices, contemplating whether to list immediately or wait until after the first of the year for a potentially higher listing.

In this business, a substantial aspect is wisdom, coupled with collaboration with other brokers. For certain listings, I provide a price range, suggesting, "I propose listing it between here and here." Concurrently, we commence the process of preparing the property, a task that may take a minimum of two to three weeks, possibly longer, depending on the season. As we approach the listing date, we revisit the comparable to identify the optimal listing price.

Bonus Section

Tips for Home Sellers

Michael LaFido:

This question is really geared towards a potential seller, whether it be their primary residence or maybe a vacation property. What advice do you have for a homeowner that is interviewing agents to sell their home?

Terry Sprague:

Firstly, it's crucial to find a broker who listens to you. Establishing a transparent and honest relationship is key, and my interviews, which often extend to two to three hours, aim to comprehensively understand my clients. After such an interaction, they might question the need to interview other brokers, given the depth of information I've gathered. I take my clients personally, delving into the driving forces behind their needs and expectations.

Understanding their expectations allows me to set realistic ones, even if it means delivering advice they may not initially want to hear. Honest guidance is something people genuinely appreciate. My marketing approach is crafted uniquely for upper-end properties, focusing on storytelling, especially for one-of-a-kind homes that may lack direct comparable. Even when dealing with more commoditized properties, I emphasize the special story behind each one.

Having worked with Forbes, I integrated my experiences from the art and auction business into my storytelling. Choosing a broker involves believing in their commitment to personally handle your case. Clients often appreciate that I am the point person throughout the process, as opposed to brokers with large teams. While some brokers have successful teams, I'm still navigating how to duplicate my approach. For now, I consider myself a bonsai tree in the realm of luxury brokers, constantly refining my methods.

Your approach should be centered on sharing best practices. When I label myself as a market leader, it's not about claiming the top spot but taking personal responsibility to innovate and elevate the standards of our delivery process. My focus is on developing new approaches, and I actively share these insights within our industry and community. Interestingly, I find myself more adept at disseminating my best practices to other brokers and firms than duplicating them for my own use. Running a small firm, more akin to a law firm with around 12 brokers, each with distinct talents, provides a valuable resource for referrals. However, I maintain a commitment to delivering services on an individual basis.

Tips for Home Buyers

Michael LaFido:

The last question I have is more geared towards someone buying a home, whether it be in their primary market or a resort market. What qualities should a buyer look for in an agent to help them decide if they should hire that agent and sign A Buyer Representation Agreement with them?

Terry Sprague:

It's intriguing to analyze my year-end business composition, with approximately 60% to 70% on the listing side and 30% to 40% on the sell side. A significant portion of the sell side involves dual agency. The remaining 20% to 25% is dedicated to working with buyers. As a listing broker, I find that transitioning into a buyer's broker role is seamless, given the insights into the techniques that drive sellers. When collaborating with buyer's brokers, I've observed a common trend where the buyer often takes the lead in the process rather than the broker.

In my approach, I prioritize efficiency and protection of everyone's time involved, including the other broker, my seller, and myself. Before visiting a property, I pose qualifying questions to streamline the viewing process. It's surprising how often I receive calls from brokers who express an intent to show 20 homes without having met or pre-qualified their clients. Working with buyers is enjoyable for me, but I insist on them following my process.

I prefer an initial sit-down to understand their architectural preferences, family dynamics, desired lifestyle, and location. Once armed with this information, I might take them to specific neighborhoods, observe their reactions to different properties, and potentially identify a suitable property on the first day. Subsequently, we may explore two to five homes before deciding. This collaborative approach, based on trust, allows me to preview properties and advise them effectively. When it comes to presenting offers, I remain old school, preferring in-person presentations, even in multiple-offer situations, with a high success rate. Representing buyers brings me joy, and I strive to make a difference by surprising and delighting on the buy side.

Visit: SecretsOfTopLuxuryAgents.com
to learn more about Terry Sprague

Connect with Terry Sprague by Scanning the QR Code Below

> **"**
> Everyone defines
> luxury different. It's all
> relative to that given
> marketplace.
> **"**
>
> Michael LaFido

CHAPTER 7

ELENA CARDONE

Author, Businesswoman, Realtor, Public Speaker, Wife and Mother. Building a Luxury Real Estate Business Through Collaboration, Networking, and Being in the Room.

ELENA CARDONE, renowned as an author, speaker, and entrepreneur, is celebrated for her expertise in real estate investing, sales training, and personal development. She is also the co-founder of the Grant Cardone Foundation and the wife of the renowned entrepreneur and real estate magnate, Grant Cardone. Together, they are parents to two daughters, Sabrina and Scarlett.

Elena's prosperous career in real estate spans various facets of the industry, encompassing investments, property management, and development. With her hands-on experience in acquiring and overseeing numerous residential and commercial properties, she has gained invaluable knowledge. Elena is committed to sharing her expertise through books, courses, and engaging speaking engagements, where she imparts wisdom on real estate investing and wealth creation. Her passion for the industry is evident in her unwavering dedication to empower others in achieving financial success through real estate.

Beyond her writing endeavors, Elena serves as the executive producer for successful events like 10X Ladies, Operation 10X Badass, Build an Empire Mastermind, and her own podcast, *The Elena Cardone Show*. Leveraging her wealth of experience, Elena has developed a comprehensive curriculum to support aspiring empire builders. Her "Build an Empire" course, designed for both men and women, equips them with the skills needed to initiate, grow, and safeguard extraordinary careers and marriages. Elena further extends her guidance through personalized coaching sessions, particularly mentoring numerous women.

Notably, Elena has forged a significant partnership with eXp Realty, earning her real estate license. Her ambitious vision is to establish the world's largest real estate team. Through this collaboration, she aspires to enable thousands of individuals to create generational wealth by tapping into the immense potential of real estate.

In this chapter of "Secrets of Top Luxury Agents," we get the chance to meet Elena Cardone, a distinguished luxury agent based in sunny Miami, Florida. As we chat with Elena, it's evident that she's dedicated to building her empire and helping others do the same. So, here she is, sharing her wealth of knowledge and insights.

Michael LaFido:

Elena, can you share the story of your very first luxury real estate transaction? Did you represent the buyer or the seller?

Elena Cardone:

Oh, that first deal was a beauty. It was a smooth $6.9 million transaction. I remember being super pumped about it. I thought, "Wow, this is a breeze, easier than real estate school!" It was a fantastic way to start my journey.

Michael LaFido:

$6.9 million for your first deal is setting the bar pretty high! I guess, depending on your brokerage, capping on your first deal means you get to keep more of the commission for the ones that follow.

Elena Cardone:

You got it. It was quite the confidence booster. But, you know, I quickly learned that not every deal is a walk in the park. There's a lot more to this business than what real estate school teaches you. So, it became crucial for me to surround myself with experts and experienced realtors, like yourself, who were willing to guide and collaborate with me until I got the hang of it.

Michael LaFido:

If you had to pinpoint one thing that sets you apart from other agents in your market, what would that be?

Elena Cardone:

Well, I have to say, my husband, Grant Cardone, and I have spent the last decade building our brand, the 10X brand. We're all about luxury and the lifestyle that comes with it. People instantly associate me with luxury, and that's a significant advantage. With the level of success we've achieved, our global presence, and the 12,000 apartments we own, it's hard to deny that we bring something unique to the table. People know us, and I leverage that to the fullest.

Michael LaFido:

What advice do you have for agents who don't have the kind of network and branding you do? How can they build their database and clientele?

Elena Cardone:

Great question. If you're not blessed with global branding like ours, you've got to work on it. Collaborate with others, and find your tribe. Take me, for instance; I've built a network of over 750 people who affiliate with my name. New agents can do the same with their own name. It's about doing the work, studying, attending courses, and learning the ropes of luxury real estate. Show up at events, make videos, and become a known expert in your niche. Utilize your existing connections and build your reputation until you stand on your own two feet with a solid track record.

Make yourself known. Send out knowledgeable information, and then people eventually start coming to you. When you build up the brand, use word of mouth and use your database full of the people you already know, that's how you start. In time you will build up the resources enough to where you can stand up on your own two feet and actually have a resume to support you when somebody asks, "What have you transacted?"

Michael LaFido:

Now, let's talk about your most memorable luxury transaction. What made it stand out?

Elena Cardone:

My first transaction is the one that will forever stick with me. It taught me the importance of understanding the property, its value, and the market inside out. I learned to predict and handle potential challenges well in advance. It set the stage for my future successes.

Michael LaFido:

How do you go about prospecting for high-end luxury clients, and what strategies have worked best for you in building your network?

Elena Cardone:

I get out there. I'm not always a fan of social events, but if it's business, I'm there. In Miami, for example, I attend the Miami boat shows, exclusive events, Art Basel, and galas for a good cause. It's a chance to meet high-net-worth individuals who are in the market for luxury properties. My advice? Get in the room, network, and seize those opportunities.

Michael LaFido:

How do you stay up-to-date with market trends in luxury real estate, and how do you use this knowledge to benefit your clients?

Elena Cardone:

I'm a globe-trotter. I travel worldwide multiple times a year, exploring properties, materials, and meeting with designers and developers. I stay on top of market trends, especially financially. Traveling internationally has given me a unique perspective on the US market, making me better equipped to guide clients. Plus, my husband runs a real estate club, where we mentor investors from all over the world, which keeps us sharp.

Michael LaFido:

How do you work with architects, designers, or attorneys to provide comprehensive services to your clients?

Elena Cardone:

In real estate, you can't do it all alone. Collaboration is key. I often seek out the best professionals in areas like landscape design, introduce myself, learn from them, and build connections. It's a win-win. Not only do you form valuable partnerships, but you also become the go-to realtor for referrals.

Michael LaFido:

Can you share some strategies for identifying and marketing to potential high-end luxury buyers and sellers?

Elena Cardone:

Agents, when it comes to networking and growing your business, there are some fantastic strategies to consider.

First, don't forget about referrals. If you know someone who could benefit from a connection you've made, send it their way. It's a great way to build trust and goodwill.

Keeping your collaborations open and transparent is essential. The more you communicate and work together effectively, the stronger your partnerships will become.

Hosting events is a terrific way to expand your network. When you attend these gatherings, it's like finding your tribe – the people who share your goals and values. They can be your support system, holding you accountable and keeping you motivated.

I've got something called "Cardone World" where we share best practices and ideas. Plus, I host a weekly 10X agent support call that's open to all agents, even if they're not part of my organization. It's all about providing value and helping others succeed.

Social media is a big player in today's networking game. It's a fantastic platform to showcase your expertise and connect with a broader audience. Don't be shy about asking for business or referrals when you've made a satisfied customer. If they had a great experience, encourage them to spread the word. It's as simple as saying, "If you were happy with this experience, tell your friends! Let me leave you a card; I'd appreciate it so much."

In a nutshell, it's all about building relationships, sharing knowledge, and being open to collaboration. These efforts can lead to a thriving network and business.

Bonus Section

Tips for Home Sellers

Michael LaFido:

What tips, suggestions, and recommendations do you have for homeowners when they are interviewing real estate agents to sell their high end or luxury home?

Elena Cardone:

The top questions that come to mind if you're a customer interviewing a realtor, are to ask the realtor how available they are to you and the project. Ask, "When do I get updates? Is it going to be you showing the home or do you pass it to one of your people in the office? What is your knowledge of this type of home? Have you done this before? What's your expertise? What's the highest property you've negotiated? What's happening in the market? What should I know about? What can I expect? What does the process look like? "

Also, I would fish around to see how excited and enthusiastic they are about the process. What do they love about your home? Why do they want your business? Do you have a strategy, does it include social media and open houses?

Tips for Home Buyers

Michael LaFido:

What questions should a buyer ask when they're interviewing agents to help them find their dream house, whether it's their primary home or a secondary home? What qualities should a buyer look for in an agent to help them decide if they should hire that agent and sign A Buyer Representation Agreement with them?

Elena Cardone:

I would find out how knowledgeable they are about the local market. Also, because of my investor background, I'd want to know the long-term investment potential of the property. For instance, if I rented it out what would the rental income be just in case I ever wanted to go down that road?

It is also important to find out how well the realtor listens. I would tell them exactly what is important to me, whether that is a view or something else, and later on in the conversation I would ask them what is the most important to me to see if they were listening. Sometimes realtors think they know what a customer needs instead of actually understanding what they want and need.

Finding out about the negotiation process is important too. I would get their take on how I can set myself up to make an offer that they cannot refuse when the time comes.

Visit: SecretsOfTopLuxuryAgents.com
to learn more about Elena Cardone

Connect with Elena Cardone by Scanning the QR Code Below

CHAPTER 8

JOHN-MARK MITCHELL

Mastering the Art of Luxury Listings

JOHN-MARK M. MITCHELL, CEO and Founder of Mitchell Forbes Global Properties, Publisher and Editor-In-Chief of Raise The Roar Magazine, and Founder of The Mitchell Academy, was recently recognized with the prestigious Billionaire's Club award, presented by Who's Who in Luxury Real Estate in Seattle, WA. "John-Mark's experience and expertise have gained him over $ 1 billion in sales throughout his career. As the only inductee in North Carolina, we are honored to welcome him into this prestigious club," said John Brian Losh, LRE® Chairman.

John-Mark M. Mitchell, a North Carolina real estate record-breaker, boasts accolades like the "Key to Our Success" from Concierge Auctions, a cover feature in the duPont Registry, and three-time winner of the "Significant Sale Award" from Who's Who in Luxury Real Estate. He also serves on the advisory board for Novant

Health and the RiverRun International Film Festival. He has been featured in Fortune Magazine, Bravo!, and A&E. He's also known for "The Art of Selling Well", and co-authored "Soul of Success" with Jack Canfield.

"The relationships we have built around the globe help our brand reach a more sophisticated clientele that demands a higher level of service in today's market. We offer an unparalleled luxury experience," says John-Mark M. Mitchell. We are committed to helping clients reach or exceed their real estate goals, we emphasize the advantages of having "A lion in your corner." Our focus is on delivering a luxury service experience and not on the price alone.

Mitchell Forbes Global Properties holds a reputation of excellence in the luxury enclaves of North Carolina with a curated collection of coveted properties that only John-Mark and his brokers can provide.

Michael LaFido:

Describe your initial luxury sale. Were you representing the buyer or the seller, and how did they come to know about your services?

John-Mark Mitchell:

One of my most memorable listings was a house called the Castle in Lexington, North Carolina. It was an amazing property with a 16-foot gated entrance and a 15-car garage on 12 acres of land manicured to perfection. The entire property was gated. The pool cost over $1 million. It's an incredible property.

I made the connection through mutual contact in the local car world. I purchased several cars from a particular dealer and of course, the homeowner with the 15-car garage was also purchasing cars, so I had established a good rapport with him. The next thing I knew, he called me to sell his house. But I had to study to make sure I put it in the right hands. So, I looked at how it had been marketed prior. Then I reached out with the resources I had and started marketing it. I also reached out to Concierge Auctions, which I'm proud to say that I now currently serve on their Board of Advisors. They marketed it to their global network and we got multiple offers. I did sell that house. Later, when the buyers called me back, I represented both the buyer and seller. Then they called me back and I sold it again. It was a triple dip.

Michael LaFido:

If you had to pick one thing that sets you apart from other agents in your local market when it comes to luxury real estate, what would that be?

John-Mark Mitchell:

The constant effort I make to be more educated in this business. I wake up every morning knowing I need to know more about what I'm doing. I think it's that drive that's behind the success we have in this company and for me personally because I really want to know more. I learn every day because the market is always changing, and so are the buyers and sellers.

The other thing I would recommend is instead of only looking at your local community, you should reach out and find mentors outside of your marketplace. Be involved in other avenues of real estate. It's the only way that you can compete with someone who has been in real estate for 10- 20 years. Just out-educate them and be more of an advisor.

Michael LaFido:

Could you recount a memorable luxury transaction that you are able to share with us?

John-Mark Mitchell:

I've had a lot, but I think the one that really stands out and had an influence on my career, was when I worked with Robert Glenn Johnson Jr., who was known as "the father of NASCAR." He is a true icon in North Carolina.

Junior Johnson was a very private man, someone who did not want a lot of hoopla. He wanted to move and had this incredible home, but he was very cautious as to how to sell it because he had other businesses. He didn't want people to think something was wrong and that he had to sell his house. The house was known as the House of Hamptonville. The highway was named after him in front of his house. He had over 100 acres and the biggest pool in North Carolina. It was an incredible estate, but we had to be cautious about how we sold it.

While I was showing Junior Johnson how we were going to sell his property, I always kept him educated as to what our next avenue was going to be. This way he always felt a part of the story and therefore, he wanted me to represent him in buying a property in Charlotte. That was an area at that time that I was familiar with, but I wasn't very active in yet. That sale opened up my opportunities, so I could branch out across the state of North Carolina and not only represent my local community.

When we found the home Junior wanted to buy, it was a multi, multi, multi-million-dollar home, so I got educated really quick. I made sure that I teamed up with someone who was very knowledgeable in that area. We worked as a team, but Junior had me as his resource and his advisor. I think that was the most memorable because it was very successful and I thoroughly enjoyed becoming friends with such a wonderful man and a great family.

Michael LaFido:

What inspired you to become a luxury real estate agent?

John-Mark Mitchell:

There are several people in my circle of influence that had been successful in real estate, but I planned to attend law school. However, I decided to get my real estate license because it would be a good addition to my law school application. Strangely enough, what I thought would be an addition to my chosen career, it became my career. I was interested in what I could do for that summer, and it turned into where I am today. The most interesting thing about that situation is that I was never inspired to sell houses. I really didn't think that would be me.

I had to find something I loved about the business and that's what I encourage people to do, find something about the business, no matter how experienced you are, that you thoroughly love. For me, it is marketing. Marketing is what I absolutely crave every second of my day. The second thing is to improve your negotiating skills because if you can out-negotiate someone, you will win.

Michael LaFido:

Share insights into your approach to prospecting for luxury clients. Which strategies have proven most effective in expanding your network within the luxury real estate market?

John-Mark Mitchell:

I have always encouraged my brokers to find what I call a Top 100. Those are the people that you can call and touch base with at least four times a year, but you're not the salesman. You're not the person that makes them say, "Let's avoid him or her because they're going to ask me to list the house."

Instead, you become the person they enjoy meeting. They know you've listened to them. You've become a part of their family. One of the hashtags we use in our company is "Let us be a part of your story." We believe that in real estate you are creating a story.

One thing that works for me is that I'm on several boards. Some of the people on my Top 100 list are on the same boards, which is nice because we're communicating in a way where we respect each other, and we work together often. I know I'm a part of their story, and that's what makes a big difference in the success of luxury real estate.

Also, get involved in your community. Find out where your community needs you, and then expand from there. Knowing more about your community and being a resource is important. I have people call me to find out what restaurants I recommend. Having that education and being a resource is a brilliant way to market yourself in luxury real estate because the experience is what it's about, they want to include you in their life.

Michael LaFido:

What's the most important skill and quality for success in luxury real estate as an agent and how have you developed these skills throughout your career?

John-Mark Mitchell:

Marketing is one. Always increase your game, do something different from everyone else, and be bold. Make sure that you're not bragging that you did $100 million last year. Instead, talk about a special house you sold or what you were able to provide for the community.

The other thing is always work on your negotiating. Of course, the more transactions you do, the better negotiator you will become.

Bonus Section

Tips for Home Sellers

Michael LaFido:

What is the number one recommendation you have for a homeowner who owns a high-end property regarding the qualities they should look for in a Realtor to sell their home?

John-Mark Mitchell:

I would ask them how many similar homes they have sold. Then, observe how they listen to your questions. Many agents don't listen. Make sure that you find an agent that no matter how successful they are, no matter how many billboards they've got, or billions they have sold, make sure they listen to what you want. I believe that observing how an agent listens to you will set you on a very good path for getting the results you desire.

Tips for Home Buyers

Michael LaFido:

What is your number one suggestion for luxury buyers interviewing agents? What qualities should a home buyer look for in an agent helping them with their home purchase?

John-Mark Mitchell:

A lot of times people think bigger is better and so they think going with an agent who has 20 people on their team is ideal. I would encourage you to proceed with caution because a lot of teams are filled with people and agents who can't cut the mustard.

I always say that the biggest producers that I've ever met have maybe two to three power players on their team and those are the people you deal with.

If you're thinking about buying a house, you want to know who the people are who will go through the process with you, because it can be stressful. Make sure you know who you're going to be dealing with and that they're going to take the time to make sure that you get the very best results in Real Estate.

Visit: SecretsOfTopLuxuryAgents.com
to learn more about John-Mark Mitchell

Connect with John-Mark Mitchell by Scanning the QR Code Below

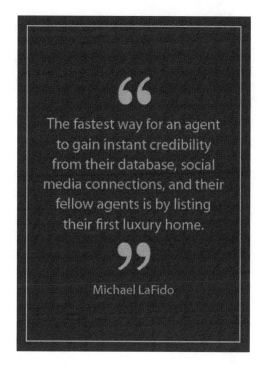

"
The fastest way for an agent
to gain instant credibility
from their database, social
media connections, and their
fellow agents is by listing
their first luxury home.

"

Michael LaFido

ROB THOMSON

Navigating High-Profile Deals
Confidentiality In Luxury Transactions

ROB THOMSON has been the top-producing agent in Northern Palm Beach County, Florida for the last 30 years. Rob Thomson carries on a legacy of excellence as the second generation among the Thomson family's three generations rooted in their family brokerage, Waterfront Properties, and Club Communities.

Thomson has sold well over $3 Billion of real estate, with plenty of records, awards, and accolades throughout his career. He has earned a coveted spot in the Wall Street Journal's Top 100 Real Estate Professionals by Volume multiple times. Beyond this, his distinctions include Who's Who in Luxury Real Estate Master Networker, recipient of the Most Referrals Award, and a membership in the esteemed "Billionaires' Club." Additionally, Rob's commitment to philanthropy recently awarded him The Florida Realtors Humanitarian of the Year for 2023 and has garnered multiple Extraordinary Philanthropy Awards, underlining his dedication to making a meaningful impact in his community of Jupiter, Florida.

Michael LaFido:

Tell us about your first luxury sale as an agent. Did you represent the buyer or the seller? How many years into the industry were you when you made the sale? How did they find out about you, or how did you find out about them?

Rob Thomson:

My first luxury sale was a riverfront property, an acre on the Loxahatchee River. When I got the listing, the owner had been dealing with a friend of his who was telling him to sell the house for a lot less than he wanted. I was willing to take it at the price he wanted. This is almost 40 years ago. For a riverfront house, he wanted $290,000. His buddy told him it was a teardown and that it would never sell for over $200,000.

But I put it up for sale for $290, 000 and I sold it to my buyer in 10 days for $280,000. The way I accomplished that price was to get the owner to do long-term, low-interest-rate private financing for the buyer.

Michael LaFido:

That's a wonderful deal you put together. What were you anxious about when you first started out? What where were you afraid of? What were the what-ifs you had in your mind?

Rob Thomson:

I don't remember being nervous. Mostly I embraced being new in the field. When I met the owner of that first property, I told him up-front that I got my license a year ago and that I had only done rentals. He said, "You're the only honest realtor I've ever met." Then he gave me the listing because of my honesty. After that, I was off to the races because he introduced me to a neighbor. I got their listing for $465,000 and sold it. I just took off from there and started being the "The Riverfront Guy."

Michael LaFido:

In addition to honesty, what is one thing you think sets you apart from all the luxury agents in your market?

Rob Thomson:

I have a large team and 24 marketing people who work here at the company. The big secret in our business is that there's no marketing department. I always tell sellers to ask other realtors if they can go on a tour of their marketing department. You're going to find out that there isn't one, that they're a high split agent. The company's getting nothing, so they don't have any incentive to get your house sold, only the agent does. I urge them to look at what we do, and I walk them through my marketing department. People are blown away by the fact that we have one and are shocked that the average agent doesn't.

Michael LaFido

Please share the most memorable transaction you've had?

Rob Thomson:

That's a tough one. We've done so many large sales, but Donald Trump Jr. is probably the most memorable because the press went absolutely crazy when that happened. The press people were blowing my phone up all day!

Michael LaFido:

That brings up a good point about NDAs. Confidentiality is a slippery slope. When you worked with Donald Trump Jr. did you have to sign an NDA? One of the challenges in our business is wanting to earn referrals, but if nobody is allowed to know you sold somebody's house, you can't leverage it as much. In this instance, if you don't mind sharing, how did that play out somehow the press did find out about the deal.

Rob Thomson:

It got out that we were working with him somehow, but it wasn't from us. I've never signed an NDA in my 40-year career. We've worked with many different celebrities, athletes, and movie stars, but we don't put it out there to the press. That said, the press has a way of finding out a lot of times.

If a client is going to record the sale in their own name, I always meet with them to let them know that It's going to hit the tax records and in 24 hours there's going to be stories about the sale. I ask them what they want my response to be when the press reaches out to me. In general, if you give the press nothing, they're going to dream up their own narrative, so the best answer is usually the truth in terms of why they bought the house. It's no big deal. It's not private information. This way they end up with a positive story instead of a negative one.

Michael LaFido:

What's the most important skill that you see consistently in top luxury agents who are successful?

Rob Thomson:

Confidentiality about people's business is important and so is being super responsive. There's no such thing as you call them back later. I answer my phone 24/7. I believe in responding to emails and texts as fast as you would answer the phone. When clients text you or e-mail you, you must respond instantaneously, not later.

The biggest thing is keeping that client's best interest in mind. I tell my clients all the time, "You can cancel this listing anytime you want, for any reason, at your sole discretion at no cost. If you decide you want to keep the house, keep it."

You don't necessarily want to sell a particular house to every person. It might be the wrong fit. Working hard, and only thinking about the client and not your commission is very transparent and super important.

Michael LaFido:

Can you share some of your best strategies for marketing a luxury home today?

Rob Thomson:

We try to hit every angle. We put all our properties in the Who's Who in Luxury Real Estate and Realm, and Mayfair International Realty out of London to get that European exposure, but we also built a huge social media following.

My advice is to build your social media by making it very interesting and high-quality. You can't do junk videos and expect quality, high-end people to want to follow you.

We do snail mail as well, including a ton of postcard mailings. I don't do magazine ads with houses in them. People don't look in magazines or newspapers for that. Also, I find internet mass email lists are critically important.

Michael LaFido:

Can you describe the process for pricing a luxury home? Talk to me about your process.

Rob Thomson:

I have a two-pronged process. First, I don't believe in talking about a price until they've signed my listing agreements.

I think the biggest trick in the real estate game is when a realtor goes to a seller's house, discusses price and condition, and wears the homeowner out discussing those two items. When this happens, you are getting off on the wrong foot. This is probably a great point for both agents and sellers. You're talking about stuff that doesn't matter. The price is determined by what buyers are willing to pay, and the condition of the home. The seller knows what he needs to do to make it the best it can be.

Michael LaFido:

How do you determine the price at that point?

Rob Thomson:

Pricing is determined by a few factors. What you must do is look at the price per square foot and what the lot's worth. Make some adjustments. But you also must have an intuitive ability to know what the property's worth.

For instance, I saw a house today where the homeowners did a beautiful remodeling job, but the home doesn't have hurricane windows and it has step-downs on the floor, which will make it hard to sell because people want everything to be on one level. The home is beautifully redone, but it still has those steps, and it doesn't have the hurricane windows.

You must be able to adjust the price and know how big of a factor certain issue will be. The only way you know how to adjust the price is by selling a bunch of them and knowing how big of a hit the other homeowners took for the same types of issues. After that, it becomes second nature.

If I were an agent that hasn't done a lot of sales yet, I would get myself either a big agent in my company to co-list it with me or I could pay them a referral for being involved in the deal. You should find somebody who has an innate knowledge of what the values are.

Michael LaFido:

Could they potentially miss out on money by choosing an inexperienced agent who underprices their services, while you, with your keen insight, could secure them a higher return than they imagined possible? Alternatively, could an inexperienced agent resort to the age-old tactic of telling sellers what they want to hear, inflating prices to secure a listing? Is this assessment accurate?

Rob Thomson:

Yes, and then the house sits on the market stale, and they could have gotten more had they priced it right when it was fresh when all the buyers wanted to see it. Now it's the house nobody wants. You just hurt your seller by giving them the wrong price.

Michael LaFido:

What channels do you use when you have an upcoming listing, and you want to reach high net-worth buyers, top-producing agents, or people who are well-ingrained and connected in the community?

Rob Thomson:

I've amassed a massive email list in different communities where we work. I have collected emails for decades for all the different homeowners in those markets, and for some of them, I have as much as 80-90% of the residents on my monthly email report. This way if a property is going on the market soon, but it's not available to the public yet, I can reach out to let select people know if they would like to see it or if they have a friend or relative who is interested, they can call me.

I've created Facebook groups to let people know what's going on too. For instance, I've created a private group for Admirals Cove, my neighborhood. Out of the 900 homes I have 500 of the residents in this Facebook group. If I have a listing in Admirals Cove, I'll start posting pictures of it before I've even listed it. In the post I let them know if they have a friend or a relative who would like to live in Admirals Cove, they can give me a call.

I get a huge response to that.

Tips for Home Sellers

Michael LaFido:

For sellers with distinctive properties who haven't sold anything in years, what advice do you have for them in terms of making their agent interviews more effective? Beyond the marketing aspect you mentioned earlier, what other tips do you have to help sellers choose the right agent, ensuring their home is positioned effectively so it gets top dollar?"

Rob Thomson:

During the agent selection process, it's crucial to approach it as a business decision. Don't hire a friend. Be sure to tell every candidate upfront that the decision is solely based on statistical data and results. Then ask each agent for their track record: recent sales, current listings, and their role in buyer and seller transactions. Eliminate agents with no buyer representation, which tells you they have ineffective marketing.

Consider how many listings they sell for others versus themselves, ensuring fair access for other brokers. Evaluate their marketing strategies extensively. Also, look at the marketing department they have. Finally, in my opinion, they should stay away from the price. It's very tempting to talk about price, but I think they should stay away from it for now and focus on marketing. Ask the agent, "What is it you're going to do to get me whatever that highest price is?"

Tips for Home Buyers

Michael LaFido:

When it comes to buying, what qualities should a buyer look for in an agent to help them decide if they should hire that agent and sign A Buyer Representation Agreement with them?

Rob Thomson:

I want to know if they are successful at getting offers accepted. Do they have access to properties that come on off-market? Will that broker pick up the phone and call everybody? Does that broker have a massive database of phone numbers and emails to reach the residents in that community? You want to know what they're going to do, not just. "Oh, I'll let you know when something comes on the MLS."

Visit: SecretsOfTopLuxuryAgents.com
to learn more about Rob Thomson

Connect with Rob Thomson by Scanning the QR Code Below

"
Don't think like
a real estate
agent. Think like
a marketer.
"

Michael LaFido

CHAPTER 10

MARIA AFZAL

Crafting Client Dreams into Realities
Beyond Property Sales

MARIA AFZAL is a preeminent name in California's luxury real estate, known for her impactful presence in the Bay Area and Silicon Valley. Maria Afzal, as the CEO of Maria Afzal Real Estate Group, Inc. and in partnership with Christie's International Real Estate Sereno, stands out for her exceptional leadership and expertise in servicing elite clients. This includes top tech executives and professional athletes from renowned teams such as the 49ers and the Warriors. Her expertise in navigating the challenging Northern California real estate market is celebrated for her professionalism and exceptional service. Maria has been designated as part of the Master's Circle, a recognition for the top 300 agents who represent more than $9 billion in annual sales.

Maria's diverse background enriches her professional approach, allowing her to effectively engage with a wide range of personalities and enhance her impressive client portfolio. Her career journey, starting in education and healthcare and transitioning to real estate, reflects her entrepreneurial spirit. Maria's quick rise in real estate started when she met her first client on the day of her obtaining her license, entering escrow just three days later. This marked the inception of her career, showcasing her exceptional negotiation skills and unwavering commitment to her clients. Today, Maria is recognized as a trusted advisor and strategic partner by all her clients.

Maria's influence extends beyond her professional achievements in real estate. As a dedicated community leader, she is the President of the Portola Valley chapter of "Together Women Rise," focusing on the economic empowerment of all women in developing countries. In her personal life, Maria values time with her daughter, a senior at Boston College, and loves traveling, especially to ancient and historic libraries worldwide. She's also a fan of pickleball. Maria and her team do more than just sell properties; they build lasting relationships that turn client dreams into realities, setting the stage for a future of continued success.

Michael LaFido:

Think back to your first luxury sale. Did you represent the buyer or the seller and how did you get the opportunity to work with them?

Maria Afzal:

My first luxury transaction was a buyer when I was facilitating an open house for my colleague at the office. Situated in one of the best parts of Palo Alto, it was an absolutely breathtaking home that I knew would sell rather quickly. I wasn't expecting to find the buyers that day especially that easily, but I continued to treat every person that walked through the door with the utmost kindness. Typically, multi million dollar homes require extensive thought and planning before completely pulling the trigger. After a few parties, a couple and their daughter walked in. They had found my advertisement through Palo Alto High School's Arts and Culture magazine. While she was still in high school, my daughter was the business manager of the program, so she'd often design my ads and put them on the magazine as a nice gesture. Although it was nice to share my business with the Palo Alto community, I would moreso pay for it to support my daughters endeavors. Their response turned to be an unexpected surprise, as a small business venture turned to foster a close community connection. It turned out that both her and my daughter were actually classmates which made it much easier to connect with the family. I am very fortunate enough to say that my first luxury transaction was exceptionally smooth, due to their immediate infatuation with the home as well as the unwavering trust I built with them. Hence, my recommendation to you all is that you never know when and where you will have a moment that will breakout your career. Do not be afraid to leverage different networks for marketing purposes as it will prove to be beneficial in some way or another.

Michael LaFido:

If you were to pick one thing that sets you apart from other agents in your local market when it comes to luxury real estate, what would that be? What advice would you have for other agents to follow in your footsteps?

Maria Afzal:

One key element that separates me from others in the luxury real estate market is my unwavering commitment to delivering personalized and tailored service to whomever my client is. There is no hesitation to put their needs above my own, clients are not only happy with the home but the price. Given that real estate is not a set salary but commission-based, many agents might selfishly focus on their benefit even if that is a bad decision for other parties involved.

Instead, I prioritize understanding the unique needs and preferences of my clients, carefully making sure that every aspect of their luxury real estate experience is curated to meet their specific desires.

My advice to other agents who are hoping to emulate my success would be to focus on building strong client relationships. Listening attentively to clients, understanding their lifestyles, and anticipating their needs can lead to unparalleled customer satisfaction. Forging good connections should be the primary step before any deal.

Ultimately, success in this niche market comes from a combination of expertise, dedication, and a genuine passion for delivering exceptional service. By going above and beyond for clients, agents can differentiate themselves and build a reputation that attracts high-end clientele.

Michael LaFido:

What are the most important skills and qualities for success in the luxury real estate market, and how have you developed these skills throughout your career?

Maria Afzal:

The luxury real estate market is tough and to excel in the industry, you must maintain a unique set of traits that transcend past the normative real estate landscape. You can't have one framework to attend to every client in every market. It is an entirely different playing field, so expect to see a change in some key attributes essential for thriving in this exclusive sector:

Real Estate is built on connection, and to sustain that you need exceptional communication skills. The ability to articulate ideas, negotiate effectively, and communicate eloquently is crucial in dealing with high-profile clients. A thorough understanding of the luxury real estate market, including current trends, property values, and exclusive locations, is imperative for providing expert guidance.

Success in luxury real estate event involves a global perspective. Understanding international markets and having a network of connections worldwide can be highly advantageous. Many buyers will be international and are looking to invest in the United States, so having that edge will put you above other real estate agents.

This will guide you on a multitude of things including which properties to buy or how to best market a home. The purchase of a home is incredibly fragile so you have to ensure that all parties are on the same page. Be prepared to participate in active listening to understand unique preferences and deliver a service that caters differently to every individual.

Mastering the art of negotiation is crucial in luxury real estate, where deals can be intricate and require finesse to satisfy both parties. While there are a couple of different negotiation strategies you can employ, find the one that works for you and go from there. There is no uniform negotiation tactic that works for everyone, so take time to invest in figuring out how that looks for you.

Furthermore, the luxury market demands meticulous attention to detail, from property presentation to transaction documentation. A small oversight in a contract or decision can have significant consequences. High-profile clients often value privacy. The ability to handle sensitive information with discretion is a key attribute.

As for personal development, successful professionals in the luxury real estate market often engage in continuous learning. This includes attending industry conferences, participating in specialized training programs, and networking with other professionals. Building a strong reputation through successful transactions, consistently delivering exceptional service, and receiving positive referrals are critical components of career development in this niche.

Michael LaFido:

What was your most memorable luxury transaction and why?

Maria Afzal:

The most memorable luxury transaction I ever had would probably be the beautiful home I sold to a 49ers player as it reflected my unwavering tenacity and hard work. It was a tremendous experience and was exceptionally thrilling making both the buyer and seller excited about this deal. Real Estate is a grueling business, especially when you work hard to uplift your career. Deals won't just be handed to your lap - you have to earn every sale you accomplish.

When my seller approached me with her beautiful Los Altos home perched on top of the mountains, I was thrilled. She had specifically chosen me as the sole agent to list her property, putting faith in my abilities to find the perfect buyer. As much as this honor came with a lot of gratitude it also came with substantial responsibility, as the seller had precise requirements: viewings strictly by appointment, adherence to rigorous house rules, and a firm decision against any remodeling investments.

Putting this house on the market was a difficult beginning, to say the least. As always, we hired a staging company to decorate the home in a way that would echo its luxurious and beautiful architecture. While I wanted it to be a seamless process, I was stunned at the initial furniture the company chose for the place.

Aesthetics are very important because it reflects a story that can be felt by those who walk into the home. The staging of any listing can either distract from the beauty of the home or amplify it. I had to call these people back and re-stage it under my instruction.

Many aspects of the home require more effort than an average-sized home. For example, I had to dedicate an hour before and after every show to open and close the property as per the seller's guidelines. With multiple showings a week, this home carved a huge hole into my schedule.

In a market experiencing a downturn in luxury home sales, I knew a conventional approach wouldn't suffice. Innovating marketing was a critical facet to pique genuine interest globally. I knew how great of an opportunity this sale was, so I made sure that it reached an international audience. With a home of this magnitude, I couldn't wait for the buyer to find me. Instead, I had to explore various avenues to identify a rough idea of who to bring the news of this home to.

One thing you will learn on the job is that every home has its distinctive attributes. As I walked across the halls and took in the views of the home in between showings, I centered on Levi's stadium from one of the patios. That's when I had a clear vision: a property with immense grandeur, privacy, and proximity to iconic landmarks, would be an excellent choice for an athlete.

A vision with no execution is nothing but an idea. I was confident that I had found a great demographic to expand my search to, but I didn't have a name. I studied some research to find potential candidates who had just moved into the area for sports.

I even embarked on a meticulously planned journey, leveraging my extensive network channel and forming a virtual team dedicated to finding the perfect match for this exquisite property. I actively went around my network finding the answer to a question I didn't even know yet. Eventually, my search helped me narrow it down to NFL players, leading me to collaborate with my trusted network in Boston.

With their guidance and my expertise in the property, we concluded who would be fit to own the home. This lengthy process trickled down to a 49ers player (top 15 in NFL), and through common connections, I met his real estate agent in Virginia. Each step involved building a virtual team focused on securing the best match for the property.

Upon returning to the Bay Area, I had a network of people within the 49ers circle to help me connect directly with the player, gaining his interest and trust. It just so happened to be, that he was already active in the housing market with a contingent offer on another home nearby.

As a realtor, I don't work for my self-interest. It is important that my clients are happy because then that makes me feel like I succeeded. Always being on top of my game, I provided the player with data-driven comparisons between my listing and the home he was considering, backed by solid evidence. I gave him my professional advice and left it to him to make the most logistical and beneficial choice.

The moment the player stood in the backyard of the home, sitting above the city lights, and caught sight of the same Levi's Stadium that brought us here, he was as amazed as everyone else was. A cheesy statement, but it was love at first sight. The escrow request was initiated immediately after this viewing, and now he is the proud owner of this luxury estate.

For me, this transaction was beyond daunting, filled with curveballs and challenging situations. It was akin to a high-stakes performance, where I had no choice but to perform with flawless execution or disappoint both the seller and the buyer. My vision, mental strength, and, most importantly, teamwork, were crucial in realizing this vision.

However, my goal extends beyond executing transactions. I am deeply committed to ensuring each deal is a win-win, fostering long-term partnerships rather than short-term interactions. This client-focused approach means working with customers over many years, across various properties, and expanding my network through heartfelt recommendations. Every home I match with a buyer is not just a closed deal; it's a testament to a relationship built on trust, understanding, and a shared vision of success.

I am a big believer in creating a mindset that pushes you to be creative and investigative in this business so that you can manifest exceptional results in turn. Without going above and beyond yourself, manifestation truly means nothing. If you make it a mission to solve the goals you have created for yourself, you won't come short.

Michael LaFido:

Can you share some strategies for identifying and marketing to potential luxury buyers and sellers?

Maria Afzal:

Certainly! Successfully identifying and marketing to potential luxury buyers and sellers in the real estate market requires a combination of targeted strategies, refined communication, and a deep understanding of the high-end clientele. Here are some effective strategies:

If you are just beginning your career, it might be worthwhile to create a circle of people you can share your listings with. Attend high-profile events, charity galas, and exclusive social gatherings where affluent individuals are likely to be present.

Cultivate relationships with professionals in related industries such as finance, law, and luxury brands who may have connections to potential buyers. Typically, listings are often sold to mutual clients.

List luxury properties on high-end real estate platforms and websites that cater specifically to affluent clients. Leverage membership in exclusive clubs or organizations to access a network of potential luxury buyers.

Advertise properties in luxury lifestyle magazines, both online and print, to reach a sophisticated and affluent readership. Depending on your location, every state has a publication that focuses on luxury real estate agents and current homes on sale.

Craft compelling narratives for each luxury property, emphasizing its unique selling points and lifestyle appeal. Host private events or exclusive property viewings for potential buyers, creating an atmosphere of exclusivity and personalized attention. Youtube is another great platform to showcase your properties. By opening your Luxury Listing to various social media platforms, you have a greater chance of finding the buyer.

Showcase your market expertise and position yourself as an expert in the luxury real estate market by consistently sharing insights, market trends, and success stories. Offer complimentary property valuations along with a comprehensive market analysis to showcase your expertise in determining the value of high-end properties.

Be active in exclusive neighborhoods and communities frequented by high-net-worth individuals, attending local events and engaging with residents. You may implement direct mail campaigns targeting affluent neighborhoods, showcasing your expertise and recent successful transactions.

Michael LaFido:

Can you describe your process for pricing luxury properties?

Maria Afzal:

While every Luxury property is different and will require its protocol, this is the process I typically enforce.

My first mission is to understand the needs of the seller. I do a complimentary meeting where I work with them to figure out their needs/wants, marketing strategies, and listing prices. While I let the other party share their insights and hopes for the sale, I give them professional advice on how to best continue the process.

Through mutual collaboration, we can make decisions on what makes sense and is best for the sale of the home. My goal is to make the seller happy by guiding them through current trends in the market, to give them a representative picture of what to expect following every decision.

1. Conduct a Comprehensive Market Analysis
2. Understand Unique Property Features
3. Assess Current Market Trends
4. Consider Economic Indicators
5. Consult with Appraisers and Experts
6. Factor in Seller's Goals and Timeline

7. Assess Competitive Landscape

8. Adjust for Market Conditions

9. Collaborate with the Seller

10. Regularly Review and Adjust

11. Marketing Strategy Alignment

By combining these steps and leveraging market knowledge, a comprehensive understanding of the property's unique features, and an ongoing assessment of market dynamics, real estate professionals can develop a well-informed pricing strategy for luxury properties.

Bonus Section

Tips for Home Sellers

Michael LaFido:

This first question is geared toward the homeowner who is thinking about selling. What should they look for when selling their luxury home? What skills, or suggestions do you have for the consumer that they should look for when hiring an agent to represent them on a sale of their property?

Maria Afzal:

That's a great question. Selling your home can be extremely emotional so finding the right realtor is critical in ensuring you have a seamless transaction. It's easy to be compelled to put all your faith in the first realtor you find, but it should take more diligence than that. This person will be your primary guide in understanding the ins and outs of selling your listing and will be dominating the marketing strategy that is put in place. Someone with inadequate experience or hard work could be the reason you lose out on a lot of money.

It's up to the homeowner to do their research and shortlist. Multiple times, I've seen out-of-area agents listing a home for way too low. The harsh reality is that every realtor can not be perfect for every home. To get the most out of your sale, I would suggest researching and shortlisting a couple of agents. Assess their portfolio and recommendations from past clients to get an accurate gist of their work ethic. Given their past experiences, question how much knowledge they have about the local market. Be investigative, be curious, and be hesitant - it is one of your most valuable purchases after all.

Review their marketing strategy, which is super important, and let me tell you why. When most people think of real estate they typically think of luxury, giving an illusion that it's pretty easy to sell. Bad news - It's not. Unlike other properties, you can't just put it on the MLS and expect it to sell itself. No - you have to go above and beyond to find creative ways of selling the home. Think advertisements, tours, and professional photography among many other aspects.

Once you have shortlisted a couple of real estate agents that you are keen to know more about, you can set up a meeting to ask the necessary questions. Asking about their past transactions is super important. Investigate how their communication and relationship-building skills are. Because how they're communicating with you is most likely how they're communicating with the buyers that are walking in, so make sure they're listening to your needs.

Negotiation skills are super important. Whenever I am on the seller's side, I strategically negotiate so that my clients can enjoy the highest purchase price possible. Discuss the realtor's approach to negotiations, especially in high-value transactions. Inquire about their success in achieving favorable outcomes for clients. Also, verify credentials and references. Any successful luxury agent should be providing a handful of references. Otherwise, that's a red flag for me.

Tips for Home Buyers

Michael LaFido:

What about your tips and suggestions for somebody who is looking to buy a home? What qualities should a buyer look for in an agent to help them decide if they should hire that agent and sign A Buyer Representation Agreement with them?

Maria Afzal:

I understand how big of a decision selling a home can be, so I empathize with my clients, putting myself in their shoes to understand their perspective. I want to be someone who will support them towards the right decisions to eventually find the right home. I always treat my clients like they are family, giving them the same advice I would give my closest friends and family.

I urge those in a position to buy a house to look for someone who will have their back, and not simply look to add another sale to their portfolio. When evaluating a potential realtor, there are several key factors to consider. Firstly, technological and marketing prowess is crucial. Can this person leverage technology effectively to uncover off-market properties?

Experience in the luxury market is another critical aspect. It's essential to assess a realtor's track record in handling high-end transactions. You need to be able to establish trust that this person will be able to perform in a way that satisfies your needs.

Additionally, proficiency in understanding property disclosures and inspection reports is vital. Homes are more than what you see in an initial showing. The history of these properties is critical to know. Your real estate agent should be able to look at these documents to highlight what you need to know to make an educated decision about whether the home is a good investment or not. Being able to identify discrepancies between seller-provided inspections and buyer inspections can save buyers from costly surprises down the line.

Visit: SecretsOfTopLuxuryAgents.com
to learn more about Maria Afzal

Connect with Maria Afzal by Scanning the QR Code Below

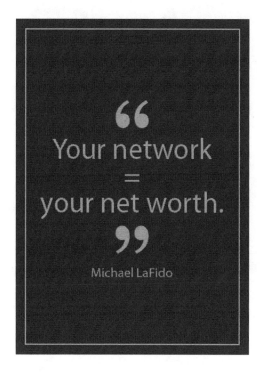

CHAPTER 11

ANTHONY DJON

The Power of Networking
Expanding Your Real Estate Reach

WITH an impressive three decades of experience in sales, Anthony Djon is a distinguished figure in the world of business. His remarkable journey has cemented his status as a nationally renowned leader, trainer, and listing specialist.

Hailing from Metro Detroit, Anthony is deeply connected to the region's vibrant community. He has left an indelible mark on the local real estate scene as the founder of Anthony Djon Luxury Real Estate, located in the suburbs of Metro Detroit. His dedication to delivering exceptional results for his clients has earned him widespread recognition and trust within the community.

In addition to his achievements in real estate, Anthony's passion for mentorship and education led to the creation of Anthony Djon Coaching. Here, he serves as a sales coach, guiding agents, teams, and brokerages to achieve remarkable growth in their numbers and success. His coaching philosophy is deeply rooted in his commitment to helping individuals flourish in all aspects of their lives.

Beyond his professional endeavors, Anthony is a devoted aviation enthusiast, reflecting his unwavering commitment to personal growth and diverse interests.

In summary, Anthony Djon's illustrious career in sales, coupled with his dedication to mentorship and coaching, has firmly established him as a celebrated national leader, trainer, and listing specialist. His unwavering passion for helping others thrive, combined with his exceptional achievements, positions him as a sought-after expert in the field of sales and real estate within the Metro Detroit community and beyond.

Michael LaFido:

Tell us about your first luxury transaction and did you represent the buyer or the seller?

Anthony Djon:

My first luxury sale was for a gentleman who was ready to relocate out of the country. He had his luxury home listed with seven other agents, but it never sold. I was the 23rd agent he interviewed to try to sell the house. That's what I was dealing with.

It was a beautiful listing in a beautiful neighborhood. But the home was severely outdated, and the seller wanted to hit a record-breaking price. That's why no one could sell it. However, after multiple open houses, and lots of money spent on marketing, I wound up selling the house after five months. I want to let you in on the level of client he was. The seller was an angry man, but here's the funny part: we would let him see the feedback and one of the comments from an agent was that the home lacked "pizzazz." Well, when he read that comment, he thought it said it lacked "pizzas," so he went postal on me. He wanted to know why I, as an agent showing his home, would think that he would offer pizzas to the buyers. It took me 30 minutes to explain it to him.

Michael LaFido:

If you were to pick one thing that sets you apart from other agents in your local market when it comes to luxury real estate, what would that be? And what advice do you have for other agents along those lines?

Anthony Djon:

What sets me apart is my extensive market reach. I have a huge database. It's largely attributed to my strong social media presence, which is local and national, and I've gained a lot of notoriety based on that.

My advice to agents is to build a strong online presence. I can't stress that enough. Your online presence must include Instagram, Facebook, LinkedIn, and Twitter. Share valuable content, engage with your audience, and showcase your expertise. And in luxury real estate, showcase your past successes. I can't say enough about that. You've got to be consistent in your social media posting and your engagement is crucial, so make sure you do it daily.

Next, you must go to the broker opens, hosted by different real estate agents. That way they know you and you know them. This is critical for your success. So is staying informed. You must keep up with the latest trends and all the developments in the luxury real estate market. This is huge and you want to share this with your followers to be known as the industry expert. I can't stress that enough either. And then obviously provide exceptional service. No amount of online presence can help you if your service is not there.

Also, you must have a lot of reviews. Ask your clients for those reviews and post them.

Lastly, you want to adapt and be innovative. You know the digital landscape is always evolving. You must stay open to new technologies and trends in our business, and you must be willing to adapt and innovate yourself to stay ahead of the competition.

Michael LaFido:

What inspired you to become a luxury real estate agent?

Anthony Djon:

I started as a buyer's agent in a very humble way. Then I advanced myself as one of the top buyer's agents locally, but I wanted more and, in our business, it's not like someone gives you a raise. I asked myself how I could get myself a raise and advance in the industry. That's what made me look at the luxury arena. I got into it, and it's been amazing for me ever since I've done that. I've enhanced my career by getting into that luxury real estate market and being on the listing side.

Michael LaFido:

What are some of the most important skills and qualities for success in the luxury real estate market? How have you developed these skills over your career?

Anthony Djon:

In the luxury real estate market, I believe several skills and qualities are crucial for achieving success. Transparency and exceptional negotiating skills are at the top of the list. Number one is being transparent and honest in all the dealings you have, not just with your clients, but also with the people that are part of that transaction.

Effective negotiating is crucial and being known as a high-level negotiator is paramount in our business.

Market knowledge is vitally important. Agents in the listing arena should have a deep understanding of the luxury real estate market, including current market trends, property values, and local market dynamics.

Then comes networking; building and maintaining a huge network of contacts within the industry like agents, architects, interior designers, and potential buyers. Knowing these people can open doors that are unique to us for referrals and lots of opportunities. I'd say another tip is to have exceptional communication skills. Being able to effectively communicate in both written and verbal form is important. You should also develop your marketing expertise and improve your ability to create a compelling marketing strategy for your sellers.

Also, adaptability is key. Make sure that you stay up to date on the latest industry changes. You never want to be behind.

Finally, patience and persistence. This is something that I can't stress enough.

Michael LaFido:

How do you manage your client's expectations to ensure that they feel informed and satisfied with the services you provide?

Anthony Djon:

I walk a client through the entire process, from beginning to end and I provide them with a clear road map. Then I address all possible issues that I think are going to come up.

Michael LaFido:

What technology and tools do you utilize to support your work as a luxury realtor, and how do you ensure that you stay ahead of the curve?

Anthony Djon:

I harness the power of social media. I use Instagram, Facebook, LinkedIn, and Twitter to showcase all our luxury properties to a global audience, which has gotten me a lot of buyers and sellers in the process. I also maintain a professional website and use it as a central hub for all my property listings, market insights, and client resources. I use virtual tours and 3D imaging.

I also count on our CR. We use 'Follow Up Boss' to manage our client relationships. It tracks communication and it maintains detailed records, which is very important for a real estate agent. Also important is data analytics. We employ data analytic tools to gain insights into our market trends. While also using market automation and collaboration tools.

We utilize a full-time tech person just to stay ahead of the curve. They research the entire industry monthly and find new technology and new systems we can employ here at my brand, and it works to a tee. It keeps our brand 10 steps ahead of everyone else.

Finally, we have a very in-depth security protocol here at the brand because we deal with a lot of high-net-worth clients. We want to make sure that all the things that we have in-house, stay in-house.

Michael LaFido:

Please describe your process for pricing unique custom luxury properties.

Anthony Djon:

My method for pricing a home is different from the way a typical agent does it. I get the client involved in the pricing from the very beginning. First, when I meet with the sellers, I'll bring my laptop with me. I'll look at the home, I'll establish a rapport with them and go through all the rooms. Then, I write down all the pros of the house and all the updates that I see. And I'm also writing down some things that could be an issue later. That's very important. Then I sit with the consumer at their kitchen table and explain we're going to price their home together and that we're going to play a little game at the end. We're going to write down what we think the house is worth on a piece of paper, and we're not going to show it to each other when we're done with everything.

I pull up all the active listings and I explain to the sellers that these are the ones that I think are going to be competition for us. What we do is we gauge if the house is nicer, or if their house is nicer? We also analyze pending listings for a dollar-per-square-foot comparison. Emphasizing closed transactions is crucial for dealing with appraisals, we note the dollar per square foot for each listing. This collaborative process helps align our valuation with the client's expectations and avoids the challenge of presenting a potentially lower estimate upfront.

Bonus Section

Tips for Home Sellers

Michael LaFido:

What are your top tips for a seller when they are considering who is best to market their home and represent them?

Anthony Djon:

When choosing a real estate agent to sell my home, I'd prioritize:

- Luxury real estate experience
- Strong understanding of the local market
- Marketing expertise
- Proven references and reviews for the agent, not just the brokerage
- Excellent communication skills and compatibility
- Exceptional negotiation skills
- Extensive networking and substantial resources
- Transparency and trustworthiness – that's the most important of all

Tips for Home Buyers

Michael LaFido:

What qualities should a buyer look for in a real estate agent, when they're interviewing agents to represent them on their purchase of a home?

Anthony Djon:

Well, a lot of the same attributes for the listing side, but number one would be experience in luxury real estate. I can't stress enough that there are big differences between the average home price and a multi-million-dollar home price.

I would look for somebody very experienced in luxury real estate. I would also look for somebody who has access to exclusive listings. It's important to ask the agent what kind of access they have to exclusive listings. I would also look for client references and reviews for this person and do a lot of research on their track record.

It's also important to find out how strong their communication skills are and if they are a good negotiator.

Visit: SecretsOfTopLuxuryAgents.com
to learn more about Anthony Djon

Connect with Anthony Djon by Scanning the QR Code Below

CHAPTER 12

WADE HANSON

Navigating Luxury Real Estate with Integrity and Innovation

FOR more than 25 years, Wade Hanson has been creating results for clients as a luxury real estate professional. His reputation for his success mindset and dedicated effort as a high performer led him to be named among Realtor® Magazine's "Top 30 Realtors Under the Age of 30" in 2005. Wade's drive and determination have paved the way for his success in a competitive industry. Wade is among the RE/MAX Circle of Legends and was also a contestant on Donald Trump's NBC television competition "The Apprentice". This experience helped Wade learn valuable business and life lessons that he treasures to this day.

A luxury market specialist, Wade has extensive expertise in marketing and selling upper-tier properties. He remains the #1 RE/MAX agent in Minnesota and Western Wisconsin; serving clients from his RE/MAX, Results office in Woodbury, Minnesota. Wade is a Certified Luxury Home Marketing Specialist, has earned the LUXE Designation and understands that marketing luxury properties is all about identifying the key characteristics that make a home unique, finding the home's story, and telling that story to the right prospects.

Wade is dedicated to cutting to the chase, making sure his clients have accurate, honest information and providing high-end service to every client. Wade's "no excuses" attitude and conviction that you must live with the choices you make drive his engaging, competitive attitude.

Michael LaFido:

Talk to us about your first luxury transaction, your first luxury sale, and do you recall if you were on the buy side or the sales side, and how did they find out about you and vice versa?

Wade Hanson:

I wish I could honestly remember my very, very first luxury sale. I've been doing this for 25 years now, so to recall my very first sale I think is challenging, but I can certainly remember one of my first.

At the time, I was selling upper bracket luxury lake homes, and I found out about a luxury gated community development that was going to be the first ever established in the area. I saw this as a unique opportunity to set my career in the upper-bracket market up for success and took the time to seek out the seller. He was from Naples, Florida, and here I am in Minnesota. I was able to reach out to him directly and took the opportunity to sell my services and myself to this developer. I think he recognized my uniqueness and one thing led to another, and I closed multiple luxury sales because of this. It turned out to be one of the greatest relationships I have to this day with a luxury buyer or seller.

Michael LaFido:

If you were to pick one thing that sets you apart from other agents in your local market when it comes to luxury real estate, what would that be and what advice would you have for agents?

Wade Hanson:

For me personally, the one thing that definitely sets me apart and makes me unique is that I really take a non-emotional, business approach to a real estate purchase or sale. A lot of agents can get caught up in the emotions of their buyers and sellers, I work really hard to make sure we can table those emotions and help my clients make good logical buying and selling decisions.

Of course, the buyer and seller, they want to love their home and be happy with their purchase. But at the end of the day, I feel that a lot of the agents really ride the rollercoaster of emotions with their clients and this often times leads to bad decision making. It's important for a good agent to be the person that can table those emotions.

Michael LaFido:

What inspired you to go into the upper price points? Some agents, they fear getting a call on a property that they have no business, maybe no experience selling. In other words, what inspired you and how did you overcome some of those limiting beliefs early on?

Wade Hanson:

What inspired me was the realization that 90% of the agents lack the effort, skills and professionalism to succeed in the luxury market. The luxury consumer demands more from the professionals they rely on. They're much, much more demanding and have higher expectations from those they do business with. I saw that I had those same high expectations of myself and I was willing to give more effort than my competitors to provide the services that a luxury consumer demands. I just think that too many agents do this part-time, they don't treat it as a professional business and they sit back and wait for things to happen. They're not that trusted advisor, they're not that consultant the luxury consumer depends on. They're just chasing that commission check. I noticed that early on in my career the high standards I had for myself matched that of the luxury consumer so it was easy for me to offer those services.

Michael LaFido:

How do you approach prospecting when it comes to luxury clients and what strategies have been most successful for you from a prospecting standpoint as well as building your network?

Wade Hanson:

I think that the prospecting aspect comes from treating the luxury consumer, buyer, or seller, like they're your only buyer or seller. You need to be available to them and get them the answers they are looking for quickly. They swim in the same waters as other luxury buyers and sellers, and they're going to refer you to their friends and family. Just making sure that you're providing a very, very high level of service to these luxury buyers and sellers is your best form of prospecting.

I know a lot of people will buy country club memberships and try to "fake it until they make it", but for me once I was able to secure that first opportunity in the luxury market, I then took things to a whole new level by providing a level of service that most agents are not willing to provide to be certain that my client had good things to say about me to others. You must be willing to be available and really be a good resource 24/7 for that client, because they're going to refer you to their friends and family. For me, my prospecting comes from referrals.

Michael LaFido:

Tell me a little bit about your network, and when we talk about networking, whether it be your circle of trust, people from a business standpoint, how have you connected with some of your most successful people in your network, referring sources?

Wade Hanson:

This just comes over time, again, and treating people with honesty and integrity and they're going to tell other people about you. You'd be amazed how quickly word travels, whether you do a good job for somebody or a poor job for somebody. Your reputation travels very, very quickly.

The community that I work in, I think with any community, it's kind of a big, small town, where it may seem big, but those that swim in those luxury waters, it's a very, very small, tight-knit community, and you've really got one chance to succeed or fail. It comes down to two words; honesty and integrity. I know its cliché, but they can see through you very quickly if you're just chasing a dollar.

Michael LaFido:

How do you stay current with market trends? Things are changing, it seems like sometimes every other week in real estate. How do you personally stay current with market trends in a changing industry, and how do you apply this knowledge to benefit your buyers and your sellers?

Wade Hanson:

It's hard, technology has forced those of us in the real estate industry to change and adapt quickly. It's becoming more and more difficult. That's one of the biggest challenges right now in today's modern real estate market, is what shiny new object are you going chase now while not getting distracted from the basics that got you to where you are. And if you're not willing to change, you can get left behind quickly.

For me it's attending seminars and different events frequently. I try to get to two or three quality events out of state every single year so that I can expose myself to other professionals in the industry that are doing things in other parts of the country that maybe we haven't implemented in my local market yet. I also think taking it upon yourself to read, listen to podcasts, to watch educational seminars online, to physically go to these seminars if you can and to network with other colleagues in the industry is important. I think tapping into others' knowledge is something you have to be willing to do.

Michael LaFido:

What are some of the most important skills and qualities for success as a luxury real estate agent in the luxury market, and how have you developed these throughout your career?

Wade Hanson:

A luxury agent should be skillful in pricing, number one, and marketing, number two, and negotiations, number three. These are three skills that are often overlooked and have certainly been overlooked in the past few years with the COVID market that we've had. You could basically price a home for one-dollar and buyers would just bid on it to create the sale price. But strategic pricing and the need to market homes aggressively are really changing quickly in the upper bracket market. Unless you're in the marketplace every day, it's very, very challenging to properly price an upper bracket home. There are so many factors to consider and so many uniqueness's to each property, it's a skill that takes time to master.

As for marketing, a lot of people say they have a marketing plan for your home, but they're really using the same plan that they've used on the $450,000 home that they sold last week. Take a few bad photos, put a sign in the yard and hope someone brings a buyer. I truly enjoy trying to secure a buyer for my listings and working both sides of the deal, so I am willing to spend the money most won't to aggressively market a home. To me, it's about identifying who you think that the buyer is for a home and really working backwards from there to compose a very strategic, very specific and targeted marketing plan for each property.

Lastly, the art of negotiations has been lost the last two or three years. During the COVID market, it was who can get to the door first and write the offer with the least number of contingencies for the highest price. There were no negotiations. There was really no "art of the deal" anymore, to steal that phrase. Negotiation is a lost art form in this industry that I think a lot of the agents that got into this business the last three or four years are quickly realizing they need to sharpen their negotiation skills. Negotiation takes patience and the willingness to walk away from a deal.

Michael LaFido:

How do you differentiate yourself and your brand in a highly competitive market? Again, and how do you maintain that strong reputation in the market as well as your referring source?

Wade Hanson:

It's funny, I just got off a phone call with a potential luxury listing right before this interview, and they were referred to me by a very well-known real estate developer here in the local market. The two words that kept coming up in our conversation were, "Well, my friend says that you're very honest and very direct." Simply being honest and direct with people is my brand and my reputation and that is going to create success in the upper bracket market (or any market for that matter) for a long time. People don't want you to blow smoke in this market. They hire you as their professional confidant just like they hire their attorney or their doctor or even their mechanic; to give them good, honest, professional advice, and they're not looking for a friend, they're looking for an advisor. A friend's going to tell you what you want to hear. A real estate advisor is going to tell you what you need to hear. By continuously doing that and creating that reputation, I think has led to a lot of success for me.

Bonus Section

Tips for Home Sellers

Michael LaFido:

This question is geared towards a homeowner, somebody that owns a house, maybe it's their primary residence, maybe it's a vacation property, but it's in the upper price points. What should they look for when interviewing agents? What's your one or two or three tips that you would have for them as to who's best to market their high-end or unique property for their given market?

Wade Hanson:

I think the consumer thinks that because we have Realtor next to our name, we're all the same. We each fly a different flag and that's really the only thing that differentiates us. The consumer needs to do their research. Too many of them are just hiring somebody because they're a friend or they're a relative, or a friend or relative recommended some person that maybe has had some success in other segments of the market. Really do your research and make sure that the agent you're interviewing understands luxury homes in your specific market.

What I mean by that is maybe somebody that lives and works in your city and their niche is entry-level townhomes, and that's okay, it's a great niche to have, but it may not be a fit for your unique, luxury home. Sellers really need to make sure that you're doing your homework, and you find somebody that works in your niche. Do they have proof of past sales in your niche? Do they have proof of a marketing plan that has worked in the past, a solid plan that's going to be specific to your property?

As mentioned before, are they just going to do the cookie cutter approach, where they take some photos, they put a sign in the yard, they throw it in the MLS, and then they hope and pray that somebody else sells your home? Or are they really going to do some print advertising, some direct social media advertising, video and online advertising that's going to reach your target audience? Or they're just trying to get a listing so that they can attach their name to it to really benefit them and their brand? It's more important than ever today to do your research on the agent that you're going to hire to sell your home, to make sure that they're capable of negotiating, marketing, and pricing your home to get top dollar.

Tips for Home Buyers

Michael LaFido:

For someone buying a property, whether it being their primary residence, primary market, or a vacation property, what qualities should a buyer look for in an agent to help them decide if they should hire that agent and sign A Buyer Representation Agreement with them?

Wade Hanson:

First and foremost, do your research, find out if you are going to be working directly with that agent or are you going to be working with a showing agent and if so, do they have the skills to negotiate on your behalf. Are they really going to look out for you in your best interests throughout the entire transaction? I'm not afraid to tell my clients, "This is a horrible purchase. You shouldn't make this purchase". And if you still want to make the purchase, go for it. But I'm going to give you the same, honest advice that I would give to my friend, my brother, my parents, whoever that might be. Sometimes a buyer needs to hear the negatives and not just the positive aspects of the home they are considering.

Some people go against my advice and that's okay. But I don't want them coming back to me in five years saying, "I want to sell my house. I wish you had told me that there's a train track half a mile from here that's going to wake us up every night." I would rather be direct with you and tell you that you're overpaying for a home, that there's going to be some obstacles when it comes to selling the home, than just go chasing a commission check.

Make sure that you do your homework. Are they willing to negotiate, do they have the market knowledge and can they clearly communicate the market values when it comes to the specific types of properties that you're looking at. A lot of agents are just walking, talking lock boxes. They're just going to go in, show you a home and sell you a home, but do they understand home values specific to the types of homes that you're looking at. I think that's one of the biggest challenges in the upper bracket market; is the ability to articulate the value of a home. I would strongly advise buyers to do your homework. This is the single largest investment you will be making in your lifetime. Is this someone you trust and do they have a team of professionals around them to help you navigate this purchase. I know I will always provide my clients with that "white glove service" every single time.

Visit: SecretsOfTopLuxuryAgents.com
to learn more about Wade Hanson

Connect with Wade Hanson by Scanning the QR Code Below

CHAPTER 13

KASTEENA PARIKH

*Building Trust and Value
The Core of Luxury Real Estate Success*

KASTEENA PARIKH is a results-driven, success-oriented, top 1% producing Houston residential broker who helps clients strategically buy and sell residential real estate throughout West University Place and surrounding areas. Since 2006, Kasteena has been the visionary behind prepping homes to sell for record prices. Her hands-on approach has ranked her as a top luxury agent in Houston by the Houston Business Journal. A lifelong resident of Houston, Kasteena's understanding of the market, coupled with her exceptional knowledge of the surrounding Houston areas, has made her the broker of choice for home buyers and sellers.

Her pre-listing services, strategic pricing, exceptional marketing program, and elevated photography and video content are essential to her consistently successful sales.

Her comprehensive pre-listing plans for design, renovation, and staging are implemented in every home she lists. Kasteena's extensive experience in design and renovation makes her uniquely qualified to advise her clients on the best investment decisions regarding which home to purchase, when to sell, and what improvements to make before selling to maximize a property's resale value dramatically. Raised in Houston, Kasteena graduated with a double major in Human Resources Management and Marketing. She was a Human Resources executive for Citigroup and American International Group before real estate. She brings a proven, unique skill set to the market, including advanced negotiation expertise, unmatched attention to detail, and a steadfast commitment to her clients.

Michael LaFido:

Can you tell us about your first luxury transaction? Did you represent the buyer side, the sellers side? And how did they find out about you or how did you meet them?

Kasteena Parikh:

I was fortunate that my first luxury sale was in my first two years of my career. I was Rookie of the Year at my brokerage. A woman who was going through a divorce visited one of my open houses. It was a house where I had spearheaded the pre-listing renovations, and the house was beautifully staged. I always have a variety of drinks and food at my open houses. I have designer soaps and lotions in the powder bath. I want my listings to feel like a five star hotel. She said she had visited 12 other open houses that day and no other agent presented their listing like I had. I followed up with her the next day and ended up listing her house a few months later. She gave me a chance and am so grateful she came to my open house that day. Since then, I have completed over 5 transactions with this same client.

Michael LaFido:

If you were to pick one thing that sets you apart from other agents in your local market when it comes to luxury real estate, what would that be? What advice would you have for other agents to follow in your footsteps?

Kasteena Parikh:

It's my passion to serve my clients and help them achieve their real estate goals - I strive to surpass all of their expectations. For sellers, I help them transform their homes and get the best return on investment. I oversee the pre-listing renovations so my listings can sell fast and for a price that breaks sales records. I almost have a sixth sense - I can walk into any home and know what it's going to take to sell the house – do we need to paint, change counters, update flooring, etc.? I have client after client who will move out of the house, relocate to whatever other house, city or country they're moving to. They will leave me the keys and credit card, and say do whatever you need to do to sell my house.

And even for new construction - guiding the builder with what buyers are looking for and getting them to trust you. I have several builders and probably one builder who is one of the most reputable builders in the area that I specialize in: West University Place - in Houston. I got him to trust me. He appreciated the collaboration so much we've become family friends. We travel with each other's families - and that's not just one builder. I have several builders where they really appreciate the service and me doing above and beyond.

For agents, my advice is to figure out what part of the business you like and build a marketing campaign around that - be consistent, don't get distracted, add value and remember it's a long game.

Michael LaFido:

What inspired you to become a luxury Realtor, and what sets you apart from other agents in the market?

Kasteena Parikh:

Prior to real estate, I was a HR executive and worked for Citigroup and AIG – we had employees regularly relocating to Houston from the east coast. When we were in meetings, I would ask them where they were going to buy, and they would let me know the house(s) that were on the top of the list. For almost every home – I knew more about the home that what they're real estate had shared with them – for example - one particularly house was just two blocks away from the animal pound, one block away from a street that was going to have a lot of future commercial development, and this street was used a cut thru during rush hour. The following weekend I toured houses with them and knew I had found my calling!

Michael LaFido:

What are the most important skills and qualities for success in the luxury real estate market, and how have you developed these skills throughout your career?

Kasteena Parikh:

Without question it's integrity and inherent honesty. A realtor must put the interests of the clients at the forefront of every transaction – it's all about the client and what's in their best interests. If you have Integrity and are authentic – people trust you and you will be successful. I learned this valuable skill from realtor Jack Cotton. In any situation where I am not sure what to do – if I ask "what's in the best interest of my client" – the answer is usually very clear. I've seen realtors not do this and the seller/buyer will tell 20 of their friends and the agent has undone years for hard work.

Michael LaFido:

How do you differentiate yourself and your brand in a highly competitive luxury real estate market, and how do you maintain a strong reputation and referral network?

Kasteena Parikh:

Branding is everything. I studied marketing and branding in college and am almost obsessed with it. People have options –how do you get them to choose you? What's your value proposition? For me, I treat every home like a brand – I love Architectural Digest and I want all my homes to look AD worthy. The photography, videography, the written word – you have to stand out from the competition. I even have an interior designer that helps me prepare all my listings including coordinating the exact furniture pieces with the staging company. Another thing we have to remember is that agents have options too - if you have a good reputation and you're known as someone who's collaborative and easy to work with - agents are going to show your homes and want to work with you and benefit both buyers and sellers.

Michael LaFido:

What unique qualities or skills do you possess that have helped you succeed as a luxury realtor?

Kasteena Parikh:

I am truly focused on elevating the client experience and embracing relationships . After being a realtor for almost 18 years, the focus is not commissions or rankings (they are important) but not my priorities. My guiding light now is the client experience and helping my clients achieve their goals. Currently, I am helping a 70-year-old relocate to Houston after losing her husband of 45 years – there are going to be a lot of hugs and tears – having the privilege of being a part of her journey brings me so much joy and fulfillment.

Michael LaFido:

What is your marketing strategy for luxury homes?

Kasteena Parikh:

Marketing luxury homes requires a specialized approach. Ask the agent about their marketing strategy and what channels they use to reach high-net-worth buyers. I've learned so many strategies from my LUXE designation training with Michael Lafido. Sellers need to understand the importance of first impressions and that the first showing is online – we have to put their best foot forward. Complete the pre-listing inspections and renovations, add staging (I am not a fan of virtual staging), take high-end photos and videos, create custom websites, and detailed amenities sheets. Buyers will pay more if they understand the added value. I use social media, email campaigns to my large database, broker open houses, and Sotheby's networking to reach buyers.

Bonus Section

Tips for Home Sellers

Michael LaFido:

What tips do you have for Sellers when choosing an agent to market their home?

Kasteena Parikh:

1. Ask agents about their marketing plan– what are they going to do to help you get the best price – will they take charge of the market preparation, pre-listing renovations, and staging?

2. Ask agents about how they work with other agents to qualify buyers. Are they abrupt and a turn off or collaborative? What is the plan for going back to buyers if there are multiple offers? Do you want an agent that's going to act in your best interest versus trying to get both ends of the deal.

3. Who is going to be showing the home? Will it be the agent, an assistant, or on a lockbox?

Tips for Home Buyers

Michael LaFido:

What qualities should a buyer look for in an agent to help them decide if they should hire that agent and sign A Buyer Representation Agreement with them?

Kasteena Parikh:

Based on the area(s) you are looking to buy, how many homes have you listed and sold?

How do you stay in tune with inventory/demand, and will you bring me listings that are not listed?

How confident are you in negotiations – especially when there are multiple offers. Have you had consistent success during bidding wars for your buyers? Recently, I had a transaction where there were 19 offers my client ended up getting, and a huge part of that was my relationship, reputation and negotiation skills with the other agent.

Visit: SecretsOfTopLuxuryAgents.com
to learn more about Kasteena Parikh

Connect with Kasteena Parikh by Scanning the QR Code Below

> **"**
> The most effective
> agents position the
> home so that the
> majority of buyers can
> envision themselves
> moving in.
> **"**
>
> Michael LaFido

CHAPTER 14

RICK JANSON

The Future of Real Estate
Integrating Artificial Intelligence for Success

RICK JANSON, owner of Rick Janson Luxury Properties, blends deep knowledge of luxury real estate with keen market insights. In recent years, he enhanced his luxury market acumen by becoming a Founding Member of REALM-Global. This recent accolade joins a long list of recognition including numerous production awards, an appearance on HGTV, and a notable mention in Forbes. Earlier in his career, the Denver Business Journal acknowledged his rising influence in 2010 with a spot on their "Forty under 40" list.

With a robust academic foundation, holding a JD/MBA in Marketing from the University of Illinois, Rick transitioned from a practicing attorney in Colorado to serving his real estate clients at a high level. His exemplary dedication was showcased in 2022, climbing to the Top 2% by production and Top 1.5% by revenue share group at eXp Realty. The following year, his industry authority was further cemented with features on the cover of Top 100 People in Real Estate magazine and Smart Agents' inaugural magazine.

A visionary, Rick founded the Power AiGENT™ Academy and serves as the Co-Chair of the AI Council at eXp Realty, steering the integration of Artificial Intelligence in real estate transactions. This innovation translates to tailored marketing strategies for sellers, ensuring their luxury homes resonate with the right audience. For buyers, Rick's AI expertise facilitates a personalized home-buying journey, aligning their preferences with ideal properties swiftly. Moreover, Rick's AI-driven insights into market trends provide both buyers and sellers with a competitive edge, ensuring informed decisions in the luxury real estate market. Through AI, Rick not only enhances real estate transactions but elevates the luxury home buying and selling experience.

Licensed as a Realtor since 2002, Rick's narrative from Lake Forest, IL to Denver in 2000 is a tale of relentless ambition. Beyond his professional life, Rick is a devoted father, passionate about photography, skiing, and travel, demonstrating a well-rounded life full of adventure. Rick's commitment to excellence has made him a leader in the luxury real estate sector, continuously raising the bar and blazing new trails.

Michael LaFido:

Share with us your first luxury sale, did you represent the buyer side or the sales side? And how did they find out about you and how did you find out about them?

Rick Janson:

At the time of my initial luxury sale, the median price point in the market hovered around $600,000. I received a call, or rather, a Facebook message, for a $1.8 million listing from an acquaintance who had been casually following my career. They noticed the value I added on Facebook, glimpsed into my family life, understood my values, and liked me as a person. Additionally, they perceived me as a local expert based on my online presence.

Despite living outside their neighborhood and acknowledging the presence of other influential figures nearby, they decided to interview me because of their positive impression. They expressed hesitation, stating that they liked me but were unsure about hiring me since I lived 20 minutes away and other notable agents lived within blocks. Their sentiment was, "You're a good guy, but…"

When I met with them, I came fully prepared, having sent my pre-listing video in advance. While I brought all necessary materials for credibility, I mainly focused on actively listening to their goals and needs during the on-site meeting. They had previously listed with a discount brokerage for 30 days and were dissatisfied with the results – facing lowball offers and unfavorable terms. What they sought was not just an enhanced marketing approach but also someone responsive to their needs.

I emphasized responsiveness during the meeting, detailing my communication plan in the follow-up. Diving deep into the marketing aspect, I avoided criticizing their previous approach but highlighted how mine would be notably superior.

Their final concern was the need for someone local to take care of their home, given their occasional absence. Addressing this, I conveyed that I was 20 minutes away by car but assured them that I would be their responsive neighborhood expert, regardless of my physical location. Overcoming the neighborhood objection, I secured the listing, and within 24 hours of hitting the market, we went under contract for just below full price. They were thrilled with the result.

Michael LaFido:

If you were to pick one thing that sets you apart from other agents in your local market when it comes to luxury real estate, what would that be and what advice would you have for agents?

Rick Janson:

What distinguishes me currently is my proficiency and utilization of artificial intelligence (AI). Upon the introduction of ChatGPT, I wholeheartedly immersed myself in this technology, undertaking every course I could find and seeking out thought leaders to become well-versed in this evolving field. Recognizing the profound impact AI would have on home sellers, home buyers, and our profession at large, I sought to position myself as an expert.

After approximately 12 months of dedicated learning, I now provide national coaching, with students across the country and around the world learning the ins and outs of AI. I believe I remain at the forefront in terms of effectively leveraging AI. Here's one way that I apply it: AI assists in identifying potential buyer avatars for a property or crafting more compelling and tailored copy that resonates with the intended audience. This isn't about discrimination, but about aligning messages with specific lifestyle preferences, home features, and neighborhood characteristics.

We utilize AI to capture these nuances and present them in a compliant and fair manner to the market and consumers, ensuring the message is compelling. Furthermore, AI aids in tracking ad spend, ensuring that advertisements across social media and other platforms effectively resonate and perform well. Thus, my fluency with AI, understanding when and how to use it, and selecting the right tools truly set me apart in today's competitive market.

Michael LaFido:

How do you stay current with market trends and changes in the luxury real estate market specifically, and how do you apply this knowledge that benefits your clients, your buyer clients, your seller clients?

Rick Janson:

The biggest asset I have in this regard is with REALM-Global. Being part of an international network of top luxury agents and being on weekly calls with them, learning from the best of the industry who feel free to fully share everything that's working in their market, everything that's working for buyers, working for sellers, working in their marketing, that free collaboration that we have with one another has been really, really beneficial. We follow trends in primary markets, resort towns or second home markets as well as international markets. and being able to stay on top of the trends, bringing in experts to speak to economics and interior design, no matter what it is that impacts the luxury home seller or home buyer, that's probably been my biggest asset and I'm just really grateful to be a Founding Member of REALM Global.

Michael LaFido:

In your opinion, what are the most important skills and qualities to be successful as a luxury agent today?

Rick Janson:

Real estate is fundamentally a relationship business, and genuine care for people is crucial. While proficiency in marketing and a deep understanding of the market are essential, what truly distinguishes you is the level of care you extend to your clients and your dedication to achieving their goals.

I believe in the adage that God gave us two ears and one mouth for a reason. During most of my listing appointments and initial consultations, I focus on asking numerous questions to understand my potential clients on a personal level and really hearing their answers. My goal is not just to be their real estate agent but to become their potential best friend, establishing a lasting connection. If I'm adding substantial value to their transaction, regardless of portfolio size, I want to become an integral part of their lives, helping in subsequent transactions and helping their friends and family. If I'm truly excelling in my role, I feel a moral and ethical obligation to extend my support to others so that they receive the best service and outcomes possible, which I know I can secure.

Approaching someone as a potential best friend fosters a long-term perspective, and genuine care for their goals is paramount. Moving isn't merely a change of residence; it's about achieving something different in life. By exploring these aspects and asking pertinent questions, I ensure a smooth, seamless, and worry-free transaction. Recognizing the uniqueness of each deal, I uncover what makes it distinct for the client. Leveraging my 20-plus years of experience, I guide them through anticipated unique situations, serving as an expert and a source of support. I stay connected, ensuring their happiness in their new home and remain ready to assist them in future transitions.

Michael LaFido:

How do you differentiate yourself and your brand in a highly competitive luxury real estate market, and how do you stay, I guess, valuable to your referral network and how do you maintain a strong reputation within your referral network?

Rick Janson:

In my early days in real estate, I set myself apart with a unique combination of skills. I held a license as an attorney, specializing in real estate and contract law in Colorado, coupled with an MBA in marketing. Adding to this, I cultivated a semi-professional hobby in photography. This blend of expertise in contracts, business marketing, and photography naturally aligned with the real estate industry. Clients were drawn to the notion that while I may not be actively practicing law, my understanding of contracts surpassed those fresh out of school, and my negotiation skills were honed across the table from other attorneys.

As my career progressed, especially in the past year, I recognized the importance of staying updated on emerging technologies, markets, and ideas. Continuous learning became a cornerstone of my approach—I attend classes regularly, seek guidance from various coaches, and recently, artificial intelligence has become a significant asset, setting me apart in the field.

Sharing knowledge is a core aspect of my professional philosophy. I provide free classes to my referral networks, real estate agents, lenders, and title companies. The belief that you can't receive with clenched fists guides me, and I've experienced that giving away information generously results in a reciprocal flow. While I can't share every piece of knowledge acquired, as it's all been taught to me, I aim to contribute faster than I receive. This spirit of collaboration extends to my interactions with title companies, representatives, and even fellow agents, fostering a culture of giving that consistently translates into referrals and new business opportunities.

Michael LaFido:

What technology and tools do you utilize to support your work as a luxury real estate agent, and how do you ensure that you stay ahead of the curve in terms of innovation?

Rick Janson:

In terms of staying ahead of the curve, I dedicate many late nights to studying, researching, and exploring advances in technology and marketing. I subscribe to numerous newsletters on AI tools, trends, and marketing, ensuring I spend 1-2 hours each day staying informed about the latest developments. The AI space alone sees 50 to 100 new tools weekly, and while I avoid chasing the shiny object, I do dive deep into vetting those proving effective. My focus is on tools that impact consumers and enhance my marketing strategy when representing a home seller.

AI can be used to address pressing concerns in the market, for example when interest rates spiked and caused "rate lock" in the market. By using large language AI models, I craft pieces that interpret these market dynamics for consumers and infuse the articles with my unique selling proposition and the target avatar.

Another favorite practice is interpreting national market trends. Rather than relying on traditional market reports, I use AI to provide consumers with actionable insights from both national and local perspectives. The specific tools I use include ChatGPT, Claude AI, Bard, and Bing, and then others for video and design. I refrain from listing all tools, recognizing the dynamic nature of the industry where tools can quickly become outdated. Staying current, experimenting with customGPTs within ChatGPT, and adapting to solve common problems in our business and for homeowners and buyers are essential practices in this ever-evolving landscape.

Michael LaFido:

What unique qualities or skills do you possess that have helped you succeed as a luxury real estate agent?

Rick Janson:

One of my unique skills lies in visual processing. During my undergraduate years, I pursued a double major in economics and studio art, satisfying both my business and artistic inclinations. While I graduated with an International Relations major, this background allows me to walk into a house and mentally remodel it, envisioning the potential of each room before leaving. If a property isn't an exact fit, I can articulate the vision of the future that I already see in my mind to paint that picture for the client. With the assistance of AI, I can now go beyond words and recreate these visions digitally as well.

The AI tools available today are extraordinary, capable of transforming a home from Scandinavian to farmhouse to rustic. This means that even if a consumer struggles to keep up visually or verbally, I can utilize AI to bring the envisioned transformation to life and say, "This is what I was talking about. Here's the potential of this home."

In the dynamic world where a home may be considered dated after just 10 years, AI becomes invaluable. It can seamlessly transition a space with cherry cabinets to a contemporary white aesthetic, or from granite to quartz, adapting to the ever-changing preferences of homeowners. Additionally, maintaining strong relationships with local builders and contractors ensures that the envisioned transformations can be executed efficiently—on time, on task, and on budget. These skills, coupled with the ability to translate visual concepts for clients, set me apart in the real estate profession.

Bonus Section

Tips for Home Sellers

Michael LaFido:

What are a few tips and recommendations for a homeowner that has a unique home, a luxury home, whether it be their primary home or a secondary market vacation property, when interviewing realtors to sell their home? In other words, what should they look for in an agent as they're interviewing to determine who's best to market and who's best to get me top dollar for my house?

Rick Janson:

Well, I believe that having strong marketing is a fundamental requirement in the real estate industry, especially in the luxury segment. Offering a comprehensive luxury package with features like a 3D model, professional photos, and high-quality video is now considered a basic standard. If a broker isn't meeting these expectations, they should be swiftly dismissed from consideration.

However, it's essential to dive deeper because distinguishing oneself goes beyond the basics. Mere access to a multitude of websites won't set a broker apart. While differences in photography and visuals are crucial – as they play a pivotal role in transitioning online viewers to in-person visitors – cutting corners on these aspects can prove costly. Opting for subpar photography, thinking an iPhone can do the job, or hiring the cheapest photographer can hinder the overall appeal of the property and significantly cost the Seller.

Once you've identified a broker who meets the standard of professional marketing, the next step is to assess their compatibility on a personal level. Given that real estate is a relationship business, understanding if the broker aligns with your values and communication preferences is crucial. Beyond testimonials, engaging in conversations with their past clients can provide insights into the kind of person you would invite into your life. Is this individual friendly, approachable, and someone you would enjoy having over for dinner? It's essential to feel confident that the chosen broker not only has the skills to get the job done but is also reliable and genuine in their commitment to follow through on their promises.

Additionally, your agent should be leveraging artificial intelligence (AI). If your listing agent isn't actively using AI in the process of selling your home in 2024 and beyond, they risk falling behind in marketing strategies, potential sale prices, and staying informed about market trends. I firmly believe that the use of artificial intelligence by your listing agent is paramount.

Tips for Home Buyers

Michael LaFido:

On the flip side of that, for someone buying a home, what qualities should a buyer look for in an agent to help them decide if they should hire that agent and sign A Buyer Representation Agreement with them?

Rick Janson:

When it comes to purchasing, several factors are crucial. Firstly, consider the amount of time you'll spend with your buyer's agent – likely longer than with a listing agent. Establishing a personal connection with your agent, ensuring they listen to your needs without being pushy, and being responsive are key aspects. The home-buying process may extend from a month to even 12 months, given current market conditions, so having a strong rapport is essential.

Your buyer's agent should also play an educational role in the process, offering insights into why an offer succeeded or fell short, providing realistic price expectations, and guiding you through the intricate details. It's important to evaluate if your agent is willing to challenge your comfort zone and not just let you dictate the entire process. While buyers may feel well-informed due to the wealth of information on the internet, a luxury agent's local market expertise surpasses that of the buyer. Trusting your buyer's agent to provide valuable input, even when it involves steering decisions in a more informed direction, is crucial. Ultimately, finding a buyer's agent who excels in their role, understands the market thoroughly, and is someone you enjoy working with is key to a successful and fulfilling home-buying experience.

Visit: SecretsOfTopLuxuryAgents.com
to learn more about Rick Janson

Connect with Rick Janson by Scanning the QR Code Below

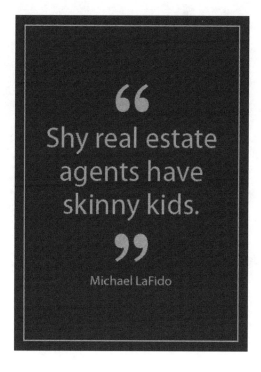

"
Shy real estate
agents have
skinny kids.
"

Michael LaFido

CHAPTER 15

TRISTAN AHUMADA

Building Value
The Core of Luxury Transactions

TRISTIAN AHUMADA operates Lab Coat Agents as its CEO, consults Fortune 500 companies, runs a successful Real Estate team in California, and expansion teams in the US (in different brokerages), is an owner in one brokerage, currently sits on different boards for tech companies, and is also an international speaker. His love for technology and systems pushes him to test and use the latest products for growth for all businesses around the world including Real Estate Agents/Brokers. Tristan is from Southern California where he currently lives with his wife and two children.

Michael LaFido:

Tell us about your first luxury sale and did you represent the buyer or the seller?

Tristan Ahumada:

I am going to tell you about the first time I did my first luxury real estate presentation.

I was sitting in an open house and I prepared ahead by making flyers that I then passed out at houses in the surrounding area hoping to pass them out to the houses in the area. One of the houses that I left a flyer for ended up calling me back. It turned out to be a $4 million home in Westlake Village, CA.

I arrived well-prepared and suited up on the scheduled day. Following the recommended procedures outlined in various books, I navigated through the home and conducted the presentation. Toward the end, they asked me, "Thank you for the presentation, why should we pay you over $100,000 in commission?"

My response was straightforward: "Because that's the commission,". Needless to say, this didn't secure me the listing or lead to a sale on the buyer's side. It was a valuable learning experience. I realized that I wasn't conveying enough value in the message that I was presenting. The fact that they had to ask, "Why are we paying you?" highlighted a gap in my approach. This encounter steered me away from luxury sales for nine years from the luxury home market. I told myself a story that I wasn't good enough for this market and it kept me away.

Michael LaFido:

Given that negative experience that kept you away for so many years, how did you transition back into luxury sales after that initial experience?

Tristan Ahumada:

I got lucky, and it's probable that many of you reading this won't experience the same stroke of luck. I urge you to step out of your comfort zone and dispel any self-limiting beliefs. The truth is, you are already capable of selling luxury real estate.

For me, the turning point came in 2015. Up until then, I hadn't come close to a $4 million sale. However, a referral from a team member led to a buyer interested in a $33 million ranch, altering my perception instantly. It dawned on me – I am good enough. Throughout the nine years preceding this realization, I had invested time in building substantial value, and now, everything I did reflected my confidence in being good enough.

That initial luxury sale served as a catalyst, opening the floodgates for more multimillion-dollar transactions. Subsequent events, like a Facebook lead turning into a $13 million sale, reinforced this positive momentum. It was a revelation for me to realize that I had been hindering my progress for years based on a self-limiting story, a lie I had been telling myself.

Michael LaFido:

What is the one thing that sets you apart from luxury agents in your market today?

Tristan Ahumada:

Transparency and truthfulness are our cornerstones. What sets our team apart is our commitment to sincerity. We won't shy away from being straightforward, telling you if selling your home at a particular price may not be feasible. However, we'll provide you with an accurate assessment based on our research. While we are open to working with your desired price, we also share the potential consequences, such as the listing expiring and cycling through multiple agents. Instead, consider our proven track record. We've assisted numerous individuals, possess extensive knowledge of the area, and are dedicated to helping you achieve your goals.

Our clients appreciate our honesty, especially at the luxury level. We understand that at this level, clients desire an agent they can trust implicitly and unload all their concerns upon, and we strive to be that trustworthy partner.

Michael LaFido:

What was your most memorable luxury transaction, and why would you call it the most memorable?

Tristan Ahumada:

Throughout my journey, I've accumulated numerous lessons, but a pivotal experience that illuminated the potential of the luxury business through online leads involved one of my agents, Luis. He successfully converted a Facebook lead I passed on to him into a substantial sale.

Initially focused on Malibu properties, the client had specific preferences. Despite this, Luis's persistence, marked by days of consistent, value-added communication (without resorting to spam), led him to propose a property in Venice, near Santa Monica. Surprisingly, they agreed to explore it.

During the home inspection, their interest extended to a neighboring property listed at $3 million. Luis adeptly facilitated the process, resulting in the purchase of both properties for a total of $7 million.

Over the subsequent five years, our relationship with this client flourished. Although their initial preference was Malibu, they eventually fell in love with a $13.5 million listing we shared via email – Matthew Perry's home. Negotiating a deal at $13.1 million, we closed it with an all-cash transaction and even presented them with a custom surfboard from Malibu. This remarkable journey began with a simple Facebook lead.

Michael LaFido:

What are the most important skills and qualities for an agent to have to be successful as a luxury agent?

Tristan Ahumada:

The paramount factor you must grasp is the intricacies of the market you operate in. A profound understanding is crucial because trust forms the cornerstone. Clients won't place their trust in you unless they are confident in your reliability for every facet related to real estate and its connections. Whether it's recommending a top-notch plumber or any other real estate-related concern, they seek assurance that they are collaborating with the best and can rely on you entirely.

Your expertise and knowledge are central to this equation. A comprehensive understanding of the area is necessary, delving into specifics like who sold a particular house, its shortcomings, and what's currently transpiring next door. Immersing yourself in the area's happenings, staying abreast of news and neighborhood dynamics, is imperative.

Moreover, don't shy away from asserting your insights into market trends. This act alone fosters trust. Many deals have materialized because we confidently communicated what was anticipated in the market, even when faced with disagreement.

Michael LaFido:

Can you share some of your best strategies for marketing?

Tristan Ahumada:

Hands down, it's targeting your audience effectively. Your audience can be in different arenas, such as agents, friends, local people who buy and sell at a similar price point, and people living in different parts of the United States and the world who can afford to buy a luxury home. You target them through social media, Google PPC (Pay-Per-Click Advertising), a newsletter, text, and phone calls.

This is where marketing online comes into play. For instance, I can go into LinkedIn, reverse prospect everybody through Sales Navigator, and target executives who live in certain areas. Now I'm going to send out different types of ads, ranging from "Check out this amazing area to live in" or "Here's an amazing home" to "Have you ever wanted to live on the beach?"

You can also go to Redfin for each area and use market insights to access all kinds of data to help you effectively reach out to people. Once you have that information, you can use it to target prospects on social media and Google.

Michael LaFido

Can you describe the process of pricing a luxury home? How have you developed a pricing strategy for unique, custom, high-end, or luxury properties?

Tristan Ahumada:

I ask the sellers in our areas how much they want for the home they are selling. Then I work backward, asking them to show me the value of the home. Who built it? What designer designed it? What architect made it?

I also consider the properties around the area that are similar in style and have the same views and amenities. If they have the same architect or designer, that helps, especially here in Malibu where we have certain architects and designers people gravitate toward. It also helps with the value of the home in Beverly Hills, Pacific Palisades, and Bel Air.

The point is, when it comes to selling luxury, I'm not just going to look to see what other homes in the neighborhood have sold for, that's the biggest mistake. I'm going to take into consideration what the sellers want and then be realistic from that point. That said, I am also willing to test out higher prices if that's what they want because they could be right.

Michael LaFido

What channels do you use to reach high-net-worth buyers or connected individuals who may know a buyer?

Tristan Ahumada:

Let's imagine, Michael, that we are agents serving the same area, and we share a solid working relationship. In such cases, I would approach you and say, "Hey, I've got something in the pipeline. I'll send you the details." The key here is that by providing information slightly before it hits the market, you are offering valuable insights to your contacts before anyone else is aware. In the luxury realm, this is akin to currency—having privileged information and sharing it early fosters a profound sense of trust.

Now, onto the second point, which agents sometimes overlook—the seller might be acquainted with a potential buyer. I engage with the seller, exploring the possibility that they may have connections in their network who could be interested. Additionally, I create compelling graphics, detailed stats sheets, or dedicated landing pages for the property. I encourage sellers to share this material with their top ten friends, either through email or text. If they prefer, I can also handle the distribution for them with the provided contact information.

Moving to the third strategy, we initiate marketing efforts on social media and Google. I also suggest leveraging "reverse prospecting" on LinkedIn, targeting individuals with the right price point who could afford the property. Utilizing this information on the backend of the algorithm proves to be highly effective. Another successful approach is maintaining a list of ultra-high-net-worth individuals. Whenever a property becomes available, we promptly share it with this exclusive group. This accomplishes two things—it informs them about the property and empowers them to spread the word. All these strategies collectively demonstrate our continued high-level performance.

Bonus Section

Tips for Home Sellers

Michael LaFido:

How can homeowners hire the right agent who will get the most amount of money from the sale in the least amount of time with the least amount of turbulence?

Tristan Ahumada:

Certainly, I have two crucial tips that are often underestimated. The first one revolves around experience, not in terms of how long a real estate agent has been in the business, but rather their networking capabilities. It's about assessing the relationships they have in place. Do they have connections with individuals who can potentially buy the home you're looking to sell?

So, my initial question would be, "What does your database look like in terms of potential buyers for my home? Are you connected with luxury agents in my area? Are you affiliated with exclusive clubs here? Who are your consistent contacts, and with whom do you engage, even beyond real estate, like during a pickleball game?" These are the inquiries that provide insights into their networking prowess.

The second tip involves asking, "How many other current luxury listings do you have at the moment?" This question isn't to gauge their experience level but rather to understand their current workload. As a seller, I need assurance that my agent will be actively involved and available. If not, they should have a capable assistant who can handle matters with the same level of proficiency. This ensures the level of service I expect as a luxury seller.

Tips for Home Buyers

Michael LaFido:

What tips do you have for somebody who is buying a unique home, or buying their first trophy property? What qualities should a buyer look for in an agent to help them decide if they should hire that agent and sign A Buyer Representation Agreement with them?

Tristan Ahumada:

In the luxury real estate realm, a crucial factor is a comprehensive understanding of the area. Suppose I were considering collaborating with you. In that case, I would expect to see a history of your extensive experience either living or working in the locality. Additionally, I would inquire about your network of real estate agents because a robust network often translates into access to off-market opportunities. In luxury, it's noteworthy that approximately one out of every three off-market homes finds a buyer off-market.

In the course of our interview, Michael, another essential aspect would be your proficiency in negotiating on my behalf. As a buyer, I might not be well-versed in various aspects, such as inspections, architectural considerations, or potential concerns related to the property's location, like being built on the side of a cliff. Therefore, your ability to guide me on what to know and what tests to conduct on the home becomes critically important in the decision-making process.

Visit: SecretsOfTopLuxuryAgents.com
to learn more about Tristan Ahumada

Connect with Tristan Ahumada by Scanning the QR Code Below

> **"**
>
> I don't have the comps to argue your price, Mr. Seller. However, I don't have the comps to support your price either…
>
> **"**
>
> Lesli Akers

CHAPTER 16

TARA MCCARTHY

From Vision to Victory
Transforming Properties for Maximum Profit

MEET TARA MCCARTHY, a powerhouse in the real estate industry with nearly two decades of experience in real estate sales, during which she has sold over 1,000 homes, approaching nearly half a billion in volume, and established herself as one of the top-producing agents nationwide.

Born and raised in Colorado, her deep local knowledge contributes to her exceptional results and extraordinary reputation as a leader in the Colorado real estate market. A bit of a self-proclaimed 'data nerd', she prioritizes in-depth understanding of not only current market trends but also forecasting upcoming changes in the market based on economic indicators. She may not have a crystal ball, but her ability to interpret market conditions and trends has served her clients well, allowing her clients to enjoy sales prices 4-7% higher than her competitors.

Tara's client roster runs the gamut, from ultra luxury property owners requiring the highest levels of discretion, to national developers, to first time homebuyers. She especially loves the challenge of taking a property in its current condition and creating a marketing strategy to maximize profits utilizing cosmetic updates. Since Tara manages the entire process on behalf of her clients, her Seller clients maximize the proceeds on every sale

with very little additional effort. Over 85% of her business is a result of repeat and referral business, a testament to the emphasis she places on a 5 star customer experience, impeccable communication, and dedication to client success.

But Tara's impact extends far beyond her impressive sales record. In addition to her work as a real estate agent, Tara is also a respected coach and mentor to other agents, particularly female Realtors. Tara is the co-founder of Girls With Grit Collective™, a community of over 17,000 women in real estate, where she is

passionate about sharing her expertise and empowering others to achieve success in the industry. Through her coaching, Tara has helped countless agents achieve their goals and reach new heights in their careers.

Tara is a sought-after speaker and thought leader in the real estate industry. She has been featured in numerous publications (such as Success Magazine's Top 100 and Success Magazine's Women of Influence) and has spoken at conferences and events across the country, sharing her expertise and inspiring others to achieve their goals.

Through her hard work, dedication, and innovative thinking, Tara has become a true force in the real estate industry. Her unwavering commitment to helping others achieve success has earned her the respect and admiration of her peers and clients alike, and she continues to be a driving force for positive change in the industry. Family plays a central role in Tara's life. Her husband & business partner Cody, and two sons Quinton & Caden, motivate her to succeed. Her favorite time with her family is spent traveling and exploring new places, or watching football from the couch all day on Sunday. Hey, life is about balance!

Michael LaFido:

Talk to us about your first luxury sale. And did you represent the buyer side, the sales side? How did they find out about you and vice versa?

Tara McCarthy:

Truth be told, my first luxury sale was completely by accident. I received a phone call from a past client connecting me with the seller of this property. It was a beautiful property on acreage. Still in close proximity to the metro area, which is pretty unique for my city.

If I am being honest, I didn't think I had a shot at the listing. I was competing with a handful of very well-known luxury agents in my area, so of which I had followed and respected for YEARS. If I approached the listing appointment on a traditional presentation competing solely on experience I would not be considered.

So, I spent a lot of time thinking about how I could bring a different perspective to the Seller, offering them a unique value proposition.

When I arrived at the property for my appointment, I couldn't help but notice how outdated it was. Every single room had cosmetic details from the 90's (or earlier), and there were several projects through the home which were half done or just executed poorly.

Up to this point a large portion of my business was flipping properties, so I had a very good eye for seeing the possibilities that a cosmetic refresh could bring to a home. I leaned into that experience and created a plan for the Sellers which involved investing a reasonable amount of money into the home and bringing it to current standards. I explained that, thanks to my background, I was able to not only create this vision for them, but also manage the entire project on their behalf.

The vision was to invest about $100,000 into the home, which in turn brought their property from an "Investor Special" into a beautifully updated estate with all the features that the current Buyers were most interested in. After showing them that the home would be worth nearly $400,000 more after the renovation, they jumped at the chance to work with me.

But that's how I earned my first luxury sale. It had nothing to do with my background in luxury sales or the previous properties that I had represented or anything like that. It was purely since I went in there with a fresh perspective on.

Michael LaFido:

We have different readers from different backgrounds, some with big companies, some with small, some newer, some seasoned veterans, some team leaders, some in Europe, some in Canada, some in Mexico, across the globe. What inspired you to become a luxury real estate agent?

Tara McCarthy:

I moved out of my house at a remarkably early age, finding myself on my own by the age of 16, residing in what can only be described as the most deplorable apartment imaginable. Picture the worst condition and location that comes to mind, and that's exactly where I was living—it was truly appalling. There were homeless people always surrounding the building, routine drug busts on the property, cars being broken into or stolen every night. It was just awful. During that time, I had just secured a position as a part-time weekend receptionist with a local real estate brokerage. I found myself providing substantial support to the brokerage owners. One of them resided in a very prestigious community here in Denver called Cherry Hills Village. I vividly recall visiting his house one day to collect some documents. Standing in the foyer, I was overwhelmed with an incredible feeling—it felt like being in a luxurious hotel. The thought crossed my mind: 'Imagine what it would be like if I were the one selling or even living in these magnificent properties.' Back then, it seemed like a distant (but possible) opportunity for me. I didn't initially enter the industry with the goal of becoming a luxury agent, but subconsciously, it had always been a goal I worked towards. We all have those distant aspirations—a dream car, an exotic trip—and for me, selling homes like those was part of that distant vision. It became something I consistently worked towards, confident that with dedication, I could achieve it. Contrary to common perceptions of luxury real estate being exclusive to celebrities and athletes, especially here in Colorado, that's not the case. Luxury real estate takes on a different meaning in this region. You could be an athlete, a business tycoon, or even a very entrepreneurial owner of a marijuana facility and be a possible luxury client."

Michael LaFido:

Let's talk about prospecting. How do you approach prospecting for luxury clients, and what strategies have been most successful for you in building your network of high-end clients?

Tara McCarthy:

There are many parallels between "regular residential" and "luxury residential." I find the thing that sets it the luxury sector apart is there's not really a one-size-fits-all approach for luxury properties. It's not like you have 10 other comparable sales to help you determine your list price. I love the fact that luxury is part art and part science. When it comes to prospecting it's all about how well you communicate your approach to your luxury marketing, particularly sellers.

Thus far, Most of my expertise has been on the listing side. Let's be honest, with a lot of these properties, their value is not something that an everyday person is going to pay for. Sellers go to great lengths to personalize their homes just to their liking, and love to have something super special about their property, especially when dealing in ultra-luxury properties. Having the ability to convey the story behind the property and helping the buyer to envision the lifestyle of the home. Naturally, skilled marketing also aids in attracting luxury buyers, right? You're proving the concept or demonstrating your expertise.

Beyond relying on my marketing to speak for me, I've discovered the true value lies in building professional relationships. Instead of directly seeking out clients, my approach involves collaborating extensively with attorneys and financial advisors. They understand that my interest isn't in merely basking in the presence of potential clients; it's grounded in my expertise and dedication to treating each client as if their deal is my sole focus. My goal is to maximize value for every client while simultaneously ensuring they receive the best possible experience. How can we achieve the highest possible return and deliver an exceptional experience for the client at the same time?

Michael LaFido:

Are you considering the long-term versus the short-term, embracing the idea of "It's a marathon versus a sprint" in the relationship and the process?

Tara McCarthy:

Certainly. It's just like you and I as people. When working with a financial advisor they aren't going to immediately deliver only their ultra-wealthy clients. They're looking for assurance that you'll be equally dedicated to all their clients, regardless of their level of wealth. This approach builds trust, and allows you to earn your way to the top of the business, right?

Michael LaFido:

What are the most important skills and qualities for success in the luxury real estate market, and how have you developed these throughout your career?

Tara McCarthy:

From the listing side, the ability to craft a compelling narrative about a property is crucial. Relying solely on the homes' specifications like the brand of the appliances or the countertops won't capture the true value of the property. Whether conveyed through cinematic video or adept copywriting, telling that story becomes paramount.

Switching gears to customer experience, I've discovered that being proactive stands out as the most vital skill in my business. Clients in the luxury price points are typically accustomed to a team working diligently for them, and they anticipate a similar level of commitment from me. Identifying issues early on and having solutions ready prior to coming Anticipating issues and solving the problem swiftly, with the least amount of financial or time loss to the client is most appreciated. They hire you for a reason. They hire you to lead them through the process. They may be super experienced within their own industry or with their own company, but many of these clients have not sold as many properties as you may expect and especially at certain dollar amounts, so they look to you for guidance.

Michael LaFido:

What technology and tools do you utilize to support your work as an agent, as a luxury agent, and how do you ensure that you stay ahead of the curve in terms of innovation?

Tara McCarthy:

Well, let's start with the fact that real estate is a bit of a dinosaur when it comes to innovation. That's the truth. As an industry, we are slow to adopt. What I strive to do is seek inspiration from other industries for different marketing techniques and technologies that may also be applicable to real estate. Staying ahead of the curve also involves continuous education, recognizing that selling a property is just a small part of an agent's responsibility. Attending conferences and being part of professional organizations, such as REALM or LUXE Listing Specialists allows me to stay at the forefront because collectively, we're better together.

In terms of tools, cinematic video is crucial. There's a significant distinction between the type of video suitable for a luxury property and what might work for a typical home in an ordinary neighborhood. Cinematic video can truly enhance the storytelling aspect. I've also discovered the impact of virtual renovation technology. The properties we represent have specific areas within the home designed for a very specific, distinct purpose. For example, the home may have a cigar room. Not every buyer sees value in a cigar room, so the ability to utilize virtual renovation technology to offer the buyer alternative uses like a wine cellar, reading room or media recording studio has proven helpful. Buyers often lack the vision we as professionals possess, so enabling them to see it for themselves, and cutting out the guesswork is valuable. However, it's important to use high-quality virtual renovation technology to avoid cheap or poorly executed visuals.

Michael LaFido:

What unique qualities or skills do you possess that you believe have helped you as a luxury real estate agent?

Tara McCarthy:

I believe, particularly for agents entering the industry, having confidence is one of the most valuable qualities. Half the battle is about believing in yourself, recognizing your capabilities, and

having the confidence to dive into the luxury market. Many agents hesitate because they feel they don't belong or lack the necessary skills. The reality is that you're likely overqualified.it. If you're passionate about it, pursue it. With determination, most of us can educate ourselves and utilize the tools available to become successful luxury agents.

My previous experience working with developers on projects ranging from 500 million to a billion dollars, has equipped me with experience in working with large dollar amounts so the financial aspect doesn't intimidate me.

The ability to confidently make sound business decisions is crucial. Assisting buyers or sellers in eliminating the emotional aspect can be immensely helpful, especially as you move into higher pricing tiers where decisions are often driven by emotions rather than logic.

Reflecting on my first deal, I've found that having construction knowledge and interior design skills has proven to be financially rewarding for my clients. Ultimately, that's what clients desire, isn't it? A greater financial gain thanks to your skills and expertise.

Michael LaFido:

What is your marketing strategy for luxury homes?

Tara McCarthy:

You've heard the saying that Lamborghini doesn't advertise on TV because those who can afford to drive Lamborghinis aren't spending much time watching TV, right? I try to apply a similar principle when marketing our luxury listings. It's about strategically identifying where potential buyers are, rather than relying on traditional platforms. You won't find someone searching for a $5 million property on Zillow in their spare time. That's not typically how it works. I start by thinking, "Where is this buyer going to be? What circles are they in? For example, I had a fantastic estate on a signature golf course, so our marketing revolved around attracting buyers who would truly appreciate the lifestyle that comes with living on one of the most coveted golf courses in the nation.

Next, I focus on the relationships I have with other real estate agents. Getting in front of the brokers and agents for buyers is crucial. When I say agents, I'm not referring solely to real estate agents but also to professionals like lawyers or representatives who assist them in navigating the purchase process. I've always enjoyed hosting unique broker opens, not the Selling Sunset extravagance, but creating meaningful events to ensure that these individuals, whether in a luxury caravan or through individual invites, are engaged. Recognizing that many clients in the luxury space are philanthropic, incorporating their charities, professional associations, and community involvement is key.

In terms of social media marketing, influencer programs can be fun and effective. Identifying community influencers, those who have a strong presence and connections in the local area, can be valuable. Individuals who know a lot of people within the community, have extensive networks, and are part of various social circles. The goal is to get the listing in front of them and entice them to share it with their community, recognizing that your buyer may not be on platforms like Zillow but connected through behind-the-scenes influencers.

Bonus Section

Tips for Home Sellers

Michael LaFido:

The next question is geared towards a homeowner that is thinking about selling, whether it be their primary residence, a vacation property. What should they look for when considering hiring an agent to sell their home?

Tara McCarthy:

Assessing your agent's capabilities and having them prove their approach is crucial even before the initial meeting. It's not just about inquiring about their follow-up plan with a buyer's agent; you can glean valuable insights into an agent's style beforehand.

What follow-up abilities has your agent already demonstrated before the first appointment? Did they promptly schedule the appointment and then maintain consistent communication, perhaps delivering a pre-listing packet in advance and following up with a video outlining marketing idea? Confirming the appointment, the day before and showing up on time illustrates a well-defined process that they likely continue. Oftentimes high ticket luxury sales have a lengthy period of consideration before the buyer commits, having an agent with effective follow-up skills is essential, making it easier to convert someone who has already seen your home.

Demanding proof of concept is also crucial. Don't settle for descriptions of videos or broker opens; ask for tangible proof. Request to see a video they've done for another property and inquire about different styles or types of properties they've marketed. This ensures you understand the breadth of their marketing knowledge.

Additionally, ask about specific properties they've represented. It's not about limiting opportunities but ensuring that the agent has experience in your price range and transaction type, demonstrating their competence in handling such deals successfully.

Tips for Home Buyers

Michael LaFido:

The next questions would be for someone buying a property, whether it be in their primary place of residence or perhaps a vacation property. What qualities should a buyer look for in an agent to help them decide if they should hire that agent and sign A Buyer Representation Agreement with them?

Tara McCarthy:

I'd suggest beginning your search by seeking referrals. If you don't have a specific agent in mind, consider agents you may know locally or those your friends and family have worked with before. A referral provides valuable insights into the type of experience you can expect, so starting there is a good approach.

For example, as part of my ongoing service to my clients who have relocated, I offer to interview their potential future agent myself, since I am obviously more experienced in what qualifications and skills are important in a luxury sale.

You also want to inquire about their access to off-market properties. In these markets, not everything is publicly marketed for sale, and understanding how source properties are not easily accessible is crucial. Ask about their professional relationships and the process they follow to locate a home that matches your criteria.

This helps you gauge whether they rely solely on MLS or explore various avenues such as connections with friends, family, professional organizations like REALM, or insights from luxury designation communities. Unlike searching for a first-time homebuyer condo, finding properties in specialized areas involves a more nuanced approach.

Visit: SecretsOfTopLuxuryAgents.com
to learn more about Tara McCarthy

Connect with Tara McCarthy by Scanning the QR Code Below

CHAPTER 17

GARY ASHTON

Crafting a Successful Luxury Real Estate Team

GARY ASHTON'S meteoric rise in the real estate realm since securing his license in 2001 has made him synonymous with success in Nashville, Tennessee. At the pinnacle with RE/MAX, he also serves as the official real estate agent/team for the Nashville Predators, signifying his unparalleled status in realty.

Originating from Leeds, England, Gary's initial foray was into music, playing with bands and exploring advertising. The turn of the millennium saw him in Nashville, reigniting musical ambitions. However, 2001 marked a career pivot when he joined Crye-Leike in Hendersonville, where he merged his advertising expertise with real estate, driving digital visibility.

2004 was transformative. Aligning with Nashville.com multiplied his leads, prompting a transition to RE/MAX Elite. Despite 2008's economic downturn, Gary's resilience kept his team dominant in Nashville. The subsequent years saw expansion, innovation, and partnerships, including an association with the Tennessee Titans.

By 2015, RE/MAX LLC recognized Gary's unparalleled contributions, inviting him to become a brokerage owner. Today, leading the world's #1 RE/MAX team and being the Nashville Predators' preferred realtor, Gary epitomizes real estate excellence with his slogan, "Don't Sell Without The Intel!

Michael LaFido:

Our first question, tell us about your first luxury sale. Did they find you or how did you find them?

Gary Ashton:

Breaking into the luxury real estate market isn't an overnight endeavor; it requires a deliberate and informed approach. My journey began with a proactive effort to enhance my understanding of luxury real estate even before securing clients. I dedicated time to exploring high-end developments, such as the exclusive gated community, LaurelBrook, located in Franklin. During this period, when new constructions were still available, I engaged with on-site agents to gain valuable insights. These interactions aimed at gathering information from listing agents and establishing a rapport with them, as they were keen on sharing their expertise, envisioning the possibility of future client collaborations.

This strategic approach eventually led to my first high-end buyer, although the initial transaction did not materialize. Nonetheless, this experience afforded me the opportunity to navigate through various subdivisions with a qualified buyer, armed with verified funds. While the buyer eventually chose a property in Charlotte rather than Nashville, the episode marked a turning point. Shortly thereafter, I received a call from a potential new general manager for the Tennessee Titans, further validating the significance of my groundwork in the luxury real estate market.

Michael LaFido:

Tennessee Titans, the NFL football team?

Gary Ashton:

Yes, I believe it was his wife who initiated the connection. During the Titans' search for a new general manager, she took on the responsibility of exploring potential relocation options. Upon learning about a potential move to Nashville for an interview, she conducted an online search for Nashville real estate, leading her to me. In our initial interaction, I successfully addressed all her inquiries, establishing a positive rapport. Following this, she mentioned that her husband, Mike Reinfeldt, would be visiting in a couple of weeks and asked if I could show him around. Mike ended up securing the job, and from being someone to show around, he transformed into my first client.

The chain of events continued as my previous client's needs aligned with Mike's, who was looking in the 2 to 3 million price range. When revisiting the same agents with whom I had interacted just a week earlier, the perception subtly shifted to my advantage. They recognized me, and greeted me with familiarity, reinforcing the impression that I had experience in luxury real estate. This unintended advantage created an atmosphere of trust and familiarity, contributing to a smoother process for Mike and solidifying my position in the luxury real estate market.

Michael LaFido:

I see you at a lot of real estate conferences. You're not afraid to travel and network, and you have a great team with systems. If you were to pick one thing that sets your team apart from other teams in your market, what would that be?

Gary Ashton:

When considering how we distinguish ourselves in the market, our team of 180 agents definitely stands out. While not all are exclusively focused on luxury real estate, we boast a robust core of experienced luxury agents. As a team, we leverage extensive knowledge and experience, bolstered by our membership in prestigious networks such as luxuryrealestate.com and remax.com. Over the past 10 to 13 years, we've been deeply involved in sports marketing, serving as the official realtors for the Predators.

This association with the Predators has been particularly rewarding, especially during a year marked by significant changes in the team, including a new general manager and numerous new players. Our clientele often seeks properties in the high-end range of 4 to 5 million dollars. Beyond traditional marketing through mediums like radio and TV, we also utilize billboards to enhance our market presence. My involvement in events like the luxuryrealestate.com Conferences has allowed me to build a valuable network, connecting with professionals like Rob Thompson in Florida and Anthony Dijon in Detroit. This extended network serves as a resource, with colleagues often reaching out when they have clients relocating to Nashville, ensuring a smooth and knowledgeable experience for those seeking our expertise.

Michael LaFido:

Talk to us about networking?

Gary Ashton:

In the realm of real estate, relationships are paramount, and this holds even truer in the luxury market. At the high end, personal referrals and connections carry significant weight alongside online leads. Often, the transition is smoother when referrals mention our team, particularly with the recognition of being the number one RE/MAX team globally. With several billion in sales over the past few years, including a consistent annual performance of around 1 billion, our experience speaks volumes.

Deborah Beagle who is my business partner, and a few others on our team who are all focused on the luxury market. What sets us apart is not just individual expertise but the collective knowledge and collaborative strength of the entire team, providing a wealth of experience for our clients in the luxury real estate market.

Michael LaFido:

That leads me kind of to my next question, and you alluded to some of that is marketing strategies for luxury properties. And you've talked about billboards, you talked about you're the preferred team or agent of the Nashville Predators, NHL, you did tons of stuff with the Tennessee Titans, you do a lot of marketing, you invest a lot of money with realtor.com and Zillow. It's not a one size fits all, but it's a combination of everything, correct?

Gary Ashton:

We have a really high profile when it comes to online presence, which I think I just explained to you that that's how we ended up working with the Titans because the general manager's wife was looking online and she found us, but also Andy Puzder, who was the CEO of Hardee's Hamburgers, which on the west coast is known as Carl's Jr., he started his search online. We ended up dealing with the relocation of all of the company from Carpinteria, which is just north of San Diego. We dealt with all those people coming over from Anaheim. They had offices in Anaheim, so coming in from California, they came to Nashville, and that was because of the presence that we had online.

Michael LaFido:

One of the things you're talking about is being found, being searchable. Before you and I even came on, I Googled Nashville luxury real estate. And guess what? You guys came up number one. You're talking about two examples of being found online and having a lot of reviews. You talked a little bit offline about how you have a system in place where when you do have a transaction, you try to obviously give a five-star experience, so that they give you a five-star review, correct?

Gary Ashton:

Expanding on that, our digital footprint is extensive. We have an exclusive 100% presence on Realtor.com, a major platform for real estate searches, which positions us as a go-to resource. When potential sellers seek exposure for their homes, realtor.com is where they turn, and we capture that market entirely. Additionally, through an exclusive partnership with Zillow, we further solidify our online reach. Prospective buyers navigating online platforms are likely to encounter us prominently.

Our websites, including NashvilleRealEstate.com and Nashville-LuxuryHomes.com, boast a strong, robust organic visibility. This strategic online presence enables us to attract inquiries and maintain a strong connection with the market. To efficiently handle the volume of business generated, we leverage technology, employing tools like Follow Up Boss to ensure seamless and effective communication.

Michael LaFido:

How do you manage all these leads? You have this large team, how do you communicate with them? Talk to me a little bit about systems, in this case, technology and Follow Up Boss is the technology that you use to communicate?

Gary Ashton:

Our platform for the real estate websites is Real Estate Webmasters. That's the foundation of how we generate businesses through SEO and having that strong presence, you've got to have a website that can actually handle that and probably getting too much into this, but the ability to rank and for Google to go, "Well, we like this. The public is having a good experience and is using the site a lot." You need a website that can actually facilitate this.

That's where we're generating a lot of the business through, as well from our online presence, and then creating that good experience for those clients that are coming from different sources, we can bring them in, and we offer a lot of benefits in terms of how often the search updates and things like that, and we tie that into Follow Up Boss. It's really maintaining that experience for the client where we're communicative, we're staying in touch. We've got systems internally to make sure that if I do give you a good lead, we're making sure that you are following up.

Michael LaFido:

Accountability, talk to us more about that.

Gary Ashton:

Accountability is something that we've set up through our Sales Director as well as all things tech! He's built some great systems to make sure that the agent maintains that relationship. When people are busy, it's not like they want to ignore that client, they want to make sure that they stay in contact. It's just having those triggers and notifications for the client and the agent. It's essentially teamwork really.

Michael LaFido:

Why did you want to get into luxury real estate?

Gary Ashton:

My approach was deliberate as I aimed to break into the luxury real estate market. The key for me was to immerse myself in those affluent neighborhoods. I made a conscious effort to explore these areas, gaining firsthand insights into the subdivisions and homes. What underscores the strength of our team is the wealth of experience and knowledge we collectively possess. Debra Beagle my longstanding business partner, and Jeff Checko, with whom I have partnered in various other real estate ventures, contribute significantly to our shared expertise. Deborah originally joined as a top agent from another brokerage, adding another layer of proficiency, and became the managing broker and my business partner, along with Jonny lee.

Our brokerage thrives on the cumulative experience of agents forming a depth of knowledge and extensive contacts. It's not just about me; it's the collaborative wisdom within the team. When it comes to inquiries on the website, it's not solely about current listings but also about having robust connections with fellow agents and builders. Understanding upcoming developments in the next six months is crucial. Striking the right balance between technology, marketing, and profound market knowledge is paramount for success in the luxury real estate realm.

Bonus Section

Tips for Home Sellers

Michael LaFido:

What are a few recommendations for a homeowner of a high-end or unique property, whether it be their primary residence or vacation property, what should they look for in an agent to represent them on the sale of their property?

Gary Ashton:

Well, it's like any time you work with a professional, you don't want somebody that's got their license three months ago. You want somebody who has knowledge and experience, and it takes time to develop that knowledge, experience, and relationships. That's not to say that somebody couldn't come on with three months of experience and also have the ability to do that. Still, I would be more inclined to look at somebody who has the qualifications, the network, the associations.

In essence, if you're thinking about who's going to be looking for your home, put yourself in the position of the buyer, how would you want to see your home? How would you have it marketed? Then I would go online and see, who's the agent that has the strong presence? Who's the agent that looks like they're selling these homes? And tour some of the neighborhoods and see who has signs in the yard. If they've got signs in the yard, that's a good agent to be talking to.

Having a great song, this is one of the analogies. If you have a world-class song and you're sat at home and you are playing that song and it's a brilliant song, well, nobody's ever going to hear that song unless you get it onto a medium that allows other people to hear that song. That's when everybody will go, "That's an amazing song." It's the same thing with real estate. If you can list the home, but you need that presence to make sure that it's not just my network that gets to see that, because obviously, we can do that, but it's on a broader scale. We want a national scale, so having a brand like RE/MAX, having the association with Zillow, having the association with Realtor.com, that's really going to maximize the exposure of the home, and then the flip side is having all those existing relationships within the current market.

Tips for Home Buyers

Michael LaFido:

Buying a property, what qualities should a buyer look for in an agent to help them decide if they should hire that agent and sign A Buyer Representation Agreement with them?

Gary Ashton:

There's a massive overlap, really you need somebody with experience. Now, my first deal, I didn't have experience, but I had people who could advise me because I would make sure I would say, "Hey Michael, I've got some clients coming in, where should I be taking them?" I was utilizing that network that I had to make sure that I was showing people the right areas, but the same thing, you want to make sure you've got an agent that has experience, I think that looking at their track record, seeing what their previous sales were, and these are all questions that it's easy to ask if you're trying to validate somebody's knowledge and somebody's experience.

That ties into the fact that we're very, very active in the luxury real estate space. We're not just doing one sale, we're doing multiple sales. Because of that, we're talking to the builders, and we're talking to other agents that are listing homes in that price range, and I think that you do, it becomes relationships and what will happen is people say, "Hey, Gary, we have a home in the $2-3M range in Franklin. It's coming on the market, and I thought you might potentially have some buyers." But again, that creates that knowledge, so as the buyer, if you're looking for a buyer's agent, you want somebody that has that network and those connections and the experience.

Visit: SecretsOfTopLuxuryAgents.com
to learn more about Gary Ashton

Connect with Gary Ashton by Scanning the QR Code Below

CHAPTER 18

PETER LUU

From Model Homes to Market Leader: A Journey to Success

PETER LUU is a distinguished figure in the real estate industry, recognized as a National Speaker, CEO, Team Leader, and Coach at Peter Luu Signature Group. With a wealth of experience as a luxury realtor in Central Florida, Peter has established himself as a prominent name in the region. Since 2016, his remarkable team has consistently Listed and Sold the most Homes in the coveted Lake Nona area, cementing their expertise and market dominance.

Notably, Peter shattered another milestone by securing the record for selling the most expensive home in Southeast Orlando in 2022. This extraordinary achievement further showcases his exceptional skills and ability to navigate the luxury real estate market with unparalleled success.

Recognized for his outstanding performance, Peter has maintained a consistent presence among the top 100 agents of Orlando since 2017, solidifying his status as one of the city's premier real estate professionals. In the most recent rankings for 2023 by ORRA (Orlando Regional Realtor Association), Peter's exceptional talent and dedication to his craft propelled him to an impressive 16th position, a testament to his unwavering commitment to excellence.

However, beyond his remarkable achievements, Peter's true passions lie in his devotion to family, community, and living a life rooted in faith.

Representing the crème de la crème of properties in the Orlando area, Peter boasts an impressive portfolio of the finest estates. His extensive client base comprises discerning individuals seeking the epitome of luxury living. From Super Bowl champions and renowned R&B artists to professional tennis players, hall of fame coaches, and wakeboarders, Peter has consistently catered to the needs and desires of high-profile clientele.

When asked about the most exciting deal he has encountered, Peter's response is unequivocal - every deal, without exception, invigorates him. Driven by his love for people, compassion, and unwavering dedication, he ensures that each customer receives the Peter Luu Signature EXPERIENCE. Through personalized attention, expert guidance, and genuine care, Peter goes above and beyond to create an unparalleled real estate journey for his clients, setting new standards of excellence in the industry.

Michael LaFido:

Peter, welcome! Could you please share the story of your first luxury transaction with our readers? Were you representing the buyer or the seller? Take us through the details of that initial deal, your inaugural luxury sale.

Peter Luu:

In my initial luxury transaction, I had the honor of representing the seller, who, coincidentally, was a builder.

Given the Orlando area's luxury real estate average price point of around a million dollars, the opportunity arose while I was stationed in a model home. Subsequently, I successfully secured a buyer for approximately $930,000.

I would like to express my appreciation to Karen, the sales consultant, for entrusting me with the responsibility to manage the model home and facilitate the sale. It was an extraordinary opportunity for which I am truly grateful.

What added to the significance of this experience was that the model home I occupied turned out to be the highest-priced property sold in the entire community. I dedicated almost a year and a half to this endeavor, consistently present from Thursday to Friday, 10 a.m. to 6 p.m. This was the pivotal entry point that led me into the luxury real estate business – all thanks to the exposure gained through model homes.

Michael LaFido:

If you had to pinpoint one aspect that sets you apart from other agents in your local market when it comes to luxury real estate, what would that be?

Peter Luu:

Branding is a focal point for me, and it's something I prioritize heavily. Those who've encountered me recognize two distinctive elements: my suit and my shoes. Within the real estate community and our local area, I've established a strong brand presence. The Peter Luu Signature Group logo, resembling the Superman symbol with the P&L initials, is prominently displayed everywhere, emphasizing the significance of branding both in our homes and personally.

An illustration of this commitment is my consistent choice to wear a suit, even in the sweltering 100-degree Florida weather. While it poses challenges, it's a deliberate effort to set ourselves apart from the competition. Our customers are well acquainted with our unique brand, reinforcing the impact of effective branding.

Michael LaFido:

Concerning branding, what advice would you offer to agents aspiring to emulate your success and establish a distinctive brand?

Peter Luu:

Consistency plays a crucial role in effective branding. Consider iconic logos like Apple or Microsoft; they maintain a consistent and instantly recognizable identity. A logo should convey meaning independently, without relying on accompanying text. The branding associated with your name and business is pivotal and should be uniform across all platforms for maximum impact.

Michael LaFido:

Can you recount one of your most memorable luxury transactions and explain why it stands out? Additionally, were you representing the buyer or the seller in that deal?

Peter Luu:

Certainly. One of the most unforgettable transactions in my career also happened to be the largest I've ever facilitated. I had the privilege of representing the seller in a remarkable six-million-dollar sale. This extraordinary property, spanning 10,000 square feet, graced the waterfront with a dock and an exquisite pool, ultimately becoming the most expensive home ever sold in Southeast Orlando. The sellers were remarkable individuals, and I successfully negotiated the best deal on their behalf.

What added a unique touch to this transaction was the personal aspect. The sellers' daughter had envisioned her wedding at the home she grew up in. Given that the listing took place in March and the wedding was set for December, we crafted a leaseback agreement with the new buyer. This arrangement allowed the sellers to retain possession of the home until January of the following year, perfectly aligning with their daughter's wedding plans. In the end, it was a deal that left everyone involved – the seller, the buyer, and especially the delighted daughter – completely satisfied.

Michael LaFido:

Moving on, how do you approach prospecting for luxury clients, and what strategies have been most successful in building your network?

Peter Luu:

Our team primarily focuses on listings, and our business is predominantly referral-based. It's true what they say – in life, your skill set, and educational background can take you to a certain level, but who you know propels you to the next level. For instance, I listed a home for a renowned college football coach, and he was referred to me by one of my past customers. This showcases that if you excel at what you do, referrals will come your way.

Michael LaFido:

In your opinion, what are the most crucial skills and qualities for success in the luxury real estate market, and how have you developed these skills throughout your career?

Peter Luu:

Consistency is undoubtedly vital, but paying meticulous attention to detail takes precedence. When entering an 8,000 to 10,000 square foot home, we consistently inquire about the seller's favorite aspects, emphasizing the unique features that set the property apart. The meticulous attention to detail is paramount.

Additionally, I'd like to offer a piece of advice to new agents – perseverance is key. If your goal is to become a luxury agent, commit both your mind and heart to the endeavor because 90% of our achievements in life are influenced by mindset. Keep pushing forward, and don't cease doing what you love.

Michael LaFido:

In terms of technology and tools, what do you utilize to support your work as a luxury agent, and how do you ensure you stay ahead of the curve in terms of innovation?

Peter Luu:

Technology plays a crucial role in our operations, particularly in refining our marketing strategies. Professional photography is non-negotiable for us – you won't find our team using an iPhone for property images. I've encountered luxury listings where lights were off, and the photographer's reflection appeared in the bathroom mirror; that falls short of our standards. We consistently engage professional photographers.

Moreover, we've embraced 3D virtual tours since 2016. Between 2016 and 2019, we successfully sold seven to nine houses each year sight unseen, a testament to the efficacy of this technology. During the pandemic, we managed to sell around 30 homes since 2020 without buyers physically visiting the property until after the inspection and contract process. Another integral technology in our toolkit is the video drone tour, enabling us to capture compelling aerial shots of the exterior and provide engaging walk-through videos of the interior, thereby enhancing the overall selling process.

Bonus Section

Tips for Home Sellers

Michael LaFido:

What qualities should a buyer look for in an agent to help them de- cide if they should hire that agent and sign A Buyer Representation Agreement with them?

Peter Luu:

First and foremost, as a seller, it's imperative to inquire about the prospective agents' marketing strategies specifically tailored to your high-end property. Seek details on how they intend to market your multi-million-dollar home and effectively reach potential out- of-state buyers. Ask if they have affiliations with prestigious publi- cations like the Wall Street Journal or Mansion Global.

Another critical inquiry involves the agent's track record in selling luxury homes. Gain insight into the number of high-end proper- ties they have successfully sold. It's crucial to collaborate with an agent possessing significant experience and a proven track record in the luxury real estate market.

Lastly, consider inquiring about the agent's team and their involve- ment in showing your home to potential buyers and their agents. Clarify whether the agent personally conducts the showings or delegates this responsibility to someone from their team. Clear communication and seamless coordination are pivotal factors for ensuring a smooth and successful selling process.

Tips for Home Buyers

Michael LaFido:

What qualities should a buyer look for in an agent to help them de- cide if they should hire that agent and sign A Buyer Representation Agreement with them?

Peter Luu:

Firstly, buyers should clearly communicate their specific needs and long-term goals to their agent. It's important to articulate what features and amenities are essential in their dream home.

Additionally, for buyers considering custom home builds, I recommend considering strategic investments and the potential resale value of the property. It's crucial to work with an agent who understands the market and can provide guidance on making wise investment decisions.

Lastly, I always encourage buyers to have a well-defined exit strategy. Understand how long you plan to live in the home and consider any potential lifestyle changes or future that may impact your housing needs. Having a clear exit strategy can help guide your decision-making process and ensure a successful long-term investment.

Visit: SecretsOfTopLuxuryAgents.com
to learn more about Peter Luu

Connect with Peter Luu by Scanning the QR Code Below

CHAPTER 19

CAROLINE GOSSELIN

Blending Technology and Tradition for Real Estate Excellence

A VISIONARY LEADER with an unyielding passion for people, marketing, and service, Caroline has propelled The Gosselin Group into one of the real estate industry's fastest-growing teams over the past decade. Her diverse team of real estate professionals spanning several states has been recognized year after year in the top 1% nationally by Real Trends.

As a connector at heart, Caroline is on a mission to redefine real estate collaboration on a global scale. Beyond working with her personal clients, she also provides consulting services to teams, guiding them in integrating effective systems and processes into their operations.

In her commitment to providing top-notch service, Caroline seamlessly integrates her expertise in serving clients across two distinct markets—New Jersey and Florida. She leverages her in-depth knowledge of New York City commuter towns in New Jersey and extends her services to the vibrant communities of Palm Beach and Broward Counties in South Florida, where she now resides.

Her involvement in community service initiatives and support for women entrepreneurs reflects her commitment to making a positive impact in every community she serves. She co-founded a local chapter of a national women's business and empowerment group (B.I.G.), held several officer roles in her local Rotary Club and has maintained steadfast support for Habitat for Humanity over the years. Recognized for her outstanding leadership, she was selected as a Top 25 New Jersey Leading Women Entrepreneur in 2019, acknowledged as a "Force for Change" by NJBiz.com in 2020, and has consistently earned her Realtor Association's Circle of Excellence Award since 2010.

Caroline's educational background includes a BA from the University of Texas at Austin and an MA in International Relations from the American Graduate School of International Relations and Diplomacy in Paris, France. Before venturing into real estate, she served as a Program Manager for a NYC-based nonprofit affiliated with the United Nations. Caroline is a devoted mother to her 16-year-old son, Lucas, who studies at The American School of Switzerland.

A dual national of France and the USA, Caroline is fluent in French and highly proficient in Spanish.

Michael LaFido:

Talk to us about your first luxury transaction. Did you represent the buyer or the seller? How did they find out about you and vice versa?

Caroline Gosselin:

Three years into my real estate career, I encountered a colleague with a distinctive British accent. He excelled at cold calling, and while he got lucky and occasionally secured a listing, he struggled to close deals. I approached him to collaborate on cold calling and our first target was a property known as "The Watchung Castle." This residence had lingered on and off the market with different realtors for several years. We met with the owners, offering an honest assessment of the market. Despite the property's stunning custom design, it was significantly overpriced and had been unsuccessfully "chasing the market." Capitalizing on the novelty of video marketing at the time, we launched an extensive Facebook marketing strategy and our efforts culminated in a line forming outside the gate at the open house. We received multiple offers on the property. This experience led me to the realization that luxury real estate wasn't inherently different. The key ingredients for success are an honest and objective look at the market and a compelling marketing campaign to distinguish the home. From that point forward, I no longer felt intimidated when approaching higher price points and recognized the value I brought to the table.

Michael LaFido:

What was your most memorable luxury transaction?

Caroline Gosselin:

It was an Arts & Crafts Bungalow - located at 27 Sagamore Rd in Maplewood, NJ. This residence holds a special place in my heart as I raised my son in this beautiful suburb of NYC.

Designed and built in 1911 by Gustav Stickley (known as the father of the American Arts and Craft movement), this property is a true historical gem. Oozing authentic character and charm, it is perched high in the hills of the South Mountain Reservation, offering breathtaking views of the city skyline.

The video showcasing the property, available on YouTube, garnered over 5K views and even caught the attention of producers at NBC's Open House NYC TV show. As a result, not one but three buyers fell in love with the property, a testament to the charm of the house, but also to my going all in in telling the home's unique narrative. I had a wonderful rapport with the sellers. They truly understood my intentions with the marketing strategy and trusted me to tell the story of the home. I represented both the buyer and seller, and those are always memorable transactions as well!

Michael LaFido:

How do you stay current with market trends and changes in the luxury real estate industry, and how do you apply this knowledge to benefit your clients?

Caroline Gosselin:

Staying well-informed about property values and market dynamics is crucial in the ever-evolving landscape of real estate. Given the international scope of many luxury transactions, possessing a global perspective and insight into international real estate trends provides a strategic advantage. To stay on top of these trends, I follow blogs, podcasts and reputable sources such as the Wall Street Journal, Forbes and Keeping Current Matters (KCM), which offer valuable insights and updates.

There's a thriving community of thought leaders committed to elevating our industry's standards. These include Brad Inman from Inman News, David Friedman at Wealth Quotient, Julie Faupel and Brennan Buckley at Realm Global, Stefan Swanepoel at the T3 Sixty Group, and Ben Kinney and Chris Suarez from Place. Those are my go to.

Attending conferences is another integral part of staying informed. Over the years, I have carefully curated which ones I attend. The Inman and Built How conferences are among my favorites. Additionally, the National Association of Realtors (NAR) and the Federation for International Real Estate (FIABCI) regularly host events that provide a wealth of knowledge and networking opportunities.

I pass along the knowledge I gain to benefit my clients through one-on-one conversations and through my newsletter distributed to both my clients and my agent network. This personalized approach ensures that my clients are not only informed but are positioned advantageously in the dynamic luxury real estate market.

Michael LaFido:

What are the most important skills and qualities for success in the luxury real estate market, and how have you developed these skills throughout your career?

Caroline Gosselin:

I often advise new agents to begin their journey by earning the Luxe certification gained by taking Michael Lafido's course. Over the years, I've maintained a list of certain skills and qualities which play pivotal roles. The list is subjective, shaped by my diverse experiences and perspectives:

Be Client-Focused & Solution Oriented: Providing personalized service is a key differentiator. You have to work to understand and anticipate the needs of your clients. As Dale Carnegie said, "To be interesting, be interested." People want to know you care.

Communication is Vital: The ability to articulate ideas, negotiate effectively, and convey complex information is crucial. Building a strong rapport with your clients contributes to a smoother and more enjoyable transaction.

Know YOUR market: In-depth knowledge of the current market trends as well as information on LOCAL property values, and market conditions, is essential. Stay informed!

Be a Connector: Building a strong network of connections with other luxury service providers is crucial. Networking can lead to valuable referrals and business opportunities. A well-connected

Realtor will have better access to exclusive listings and may be aware of off-market opportunities.

Trust is Paramount: Clients need to feel confident that their agent has their best interests at heart and can be trusted with sensitive information. High-net-worth individuals value their privacy. Being discreet and maintaining confidentiality is essential in the luxury real estate market.

Devil is in the Details: The luxury market demands a high level of attention to detail. Every aspect of a transaction, from marketing materials to property presentations, must be meticulously handled.

Be Adaptable, Patient and Persistent: The market can be dynamic and subject to changes in economic conditions and client preferences - you have to adapt and adjust your strategies accordingly. Patience and persistence are crucial qualities.

Be Culturally Competent: Dealing with a diverse clientele requires cultural competence. Understanding and respecting different cultural norms and expectations can contribute to successful interactions and building trust and rapport.

Michael LaFido:

What technology and tools do you utilize to support your work as a luxury realtor, and how do you ensure that you stay ahead of the curve in terms of innovation?

Caroline Gosselin:

Maintaining momentum in this industry demands an innate interest in technology and innovation. Over the past decade, the industry has witnessed a transformation, shaping a modern real estate landscape marked by the pervasive use of digital tools and the game-changing influence of AI. While the common sentiment is that Realtors won't be replaced by AI, it's believed that Realtors using AI will replace the average Realtor. Personally, I've always embraced new technologies, whether they streamline my personal or business goals. Our team leverages a suite of tools:

- **Google Business Suite:** Essential for emails and fostering collaboration through shared calendars.

- **Slack:** Communication platform for the team.

- **Brivity CRM:** Centralized hub for client information, task management, and transaction details.

- **Skyslope:** Handles our document management and facilitates electronic signatures for a more efficient and secure process.

- **Canva:** It allows us to share customizable graphic templates across the team.

- **Chat GPT:** We plan to utilize this tool more this year for inquiries, content creation, market research, and training.

- **Blockchain Technology:** I plan to delve into its applications in 2024 to enhance client security and transparency in our transactions.

This continual integration of innovative tools reflects our commitment to staying at the forefront of the industry. Our goal is to offer clients an exceptional and technologically advanced real estate experience.

Michael LaFido:

How do you work with other professionals in your inner circle such as your interior designers, decorators, stagers, attorneys, as your strategic partners?

Caroline Gosselin:

Great realtors are, at their core, connectors. In this business, collaboration across various industries is essential to provide clients with a comprehensive solution. The timing of involving other professionals, be they inspectors, architects, designers, contractors, builders, or attorneys depends on the specific timeline and scope of a clients' plans. To truly grasp a client's vision and goals, I always start with an initial consultation and needs assessment.

What I've discovered to be paramount is collaborating with professionals who share the same work ethic. No divas are allowed! Effective communication, mutual respect, and a clear understanding of our professional roles are essential for successful collaboration across our disciplines. As I mentioned initially, great realtors excel at bringing together all the pieces of the puzzle.

Michael LaFido:

How do you balance providing personalized attention to your clients by still managing multiple high value listings all at once?

Caroline Gosselin:

With a simple yet powerful 4-letter word: T-E-A-M. It's no secret that success in our industry is about leveraging the collaborative efforts of a team. When I started in real estate over 15 years ago, I saw pretty early on that teams were going to be the future of the industry. I think it is all about understanding your strengths and weaknesses, leveraging people's skills and building a team around that. Teams can be very fluid. People have different iterations of teams over time - I certainly have.

I've had the privilege of having a dedicated Chief of Operations over the years and we've embraced the efficiency of Virtual Assistants. The impact they make is truly remarkable. Ultimately, pulling together the right team and making sure everyone understands their roles, stands out as the most important factor. It is this cohesive unit that forms the backbone of successful operations, allowing us to provide top-notch service consistently.

Bonus Section

Tips for Home Sellers

Michael LaFido:

What are a few tips and recommendations for owners of a luxury home who are interviewing Realtors to sell their home?

Caroline Gosselin:

- Do your research. Do YOU find their marketing compelling? Does it resonate with YOU?

- Do they utilize video marketing at a high-level?

- Ask the agent what networks they will be leveraging to market your property?

- Are they willing to share references?

- Ask to see customized marketing plans for your particular property.

Tips for Home Buyers

Michael LaFido:

What qualities should a buyer look for in an agent to help them decide if they should hire that agent and sign A Buyer Representation Agreement with them?

Caroline Gosselin:

A well-connected Realtor will have access to exclusive listings and off-market opportunities. Ask how they will communicate those to you.

Is the agent willing to share references or past client testimonials?

Expect a Realtor to be responsive and communicative with you. A home search can be time-consuming, so it's important to work with someone who is willing to go the long-haul with you.

Personal compatibility should not be discounted. Building a strong rapport and feeling comfortable with your Realtor can contribute to a smoother and more enjoyable home-buying experience.

Visit: SecretsOfTopLuxuryAgents.com
to learn more about Caroline Gosselin

Connect with Caroline Gosselin by Scanning the QR Code Below

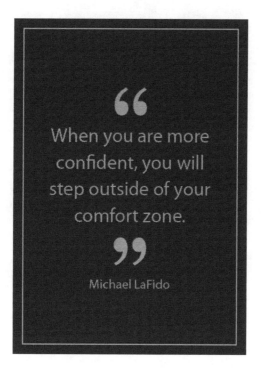

> **"**
> When you are more
> confident, you will
> step outside of your
> comfort zone.
> **"**
>
> Michael LaFido

CHAPTER 20

PAUL CAMPANO

*Innovation and Personal Touch
Balancing High-Net-Worth Client Needs*

IN A CITY where luxury and history converge on the edges of affluent and blue color neighborhoods, the upper echelon of high-end real estate sales know a common name - Paul Campano. For nearly the last two decades and essentially half of his life, Paul has dedicated his career to the discovery and advocacy of unique property, and his hundreds of millions in closed sales prove his passion and curiosity, coupled with his unwavering advocacy for

His clients are the royal road to Boston real estate success. Boston is a city where local flavor and the historic one-way cobblestone roads aren't the only challenge to navigate. Raised in a triple decker Somerville home that his grandmother purchased for $24k, Paul knew from childhood that hard work wasn't optional and networking these insular Boston neighbors were his path to creating something special and so Paul went "all-in" on his neighborhood roots. As a product of Somerville public schools, he went on to attend Suffolk University as an Archer

Fellow....the highest academic honor the University conveys. He was also an undefeated varsity athlete on the mound bringing that competitive spirit to one of the most competitive real estate markets in the world. After the unexpected passing of his father, Paul made the difficult decision to leave school and work on the technology side of a real estate start-up which was soon acquired, giving him a taste for business and development and all the ingredients of what it means to navigate Greater Boston's B2B landscape. Paul's father taught him to work hard and to always pursue his goals, concepts which live on his Paul's day to day

innovative approach to marketing and relationship-building, which has fueled countless record-breaking sales in Boston proper and beyond. He believes that the most successful entrepreneurs and realtors are well rounded not just as business people but as people. And so Paul enjoys giving back. He was one of 30 inaugural "Real Men Making Strides" along with Mayor Walsh, Governor Baker and other notable Bostonians in the fight against Breast Cancer. He also was the first Realtor is Massachusetts to partner with Homes for Heroes....offering discounts and benefits to First Responders and Health care workers as Paul believes and lives "Boston Strong." Most recently, Paul has been the unofficial go-to for athletes moving to the Boston area,supporting a group who have earned contracts collectively in excess of 1 Billion Dollars. Paul's advisement has been instrumental in continuing their success off the court and field into real estate.

Michael LaFido:

I want to ask you about your first luxury sale. Did you represent the buyer or the seller? How did they find out about you and vice versa?

Paul Campano:

In my first luxury sale, I represented the seller—a developer with a distinctive vision. The journey began when I had a buyer in search of a truly unique property. After exploring various options on the market, my client pointed to an abandoned mill building, expressing a desire for a blank canvas—a space where he could craft his own masterpiece.

Although the initial building didn't meet all the buyer's criteria, I had to dig deeper. I researched and tracked down numerous distinctive buildings across Greater Boston. One such property was an abandoned firehouse, untouched for decades. While my clients ultimately decided to pass on this one, I established a connection with the owner.

Over the following 11 months, I continually checked in with the owner. Whether through calls, letters, or site visits, I remained engaged with his project. Even during specific challenges, like countertop issues and custom hardwood milling in Canada, I stayed in the loop and offered support.

When the developer finally completed the project, he invited me for an extensive tour. Subsequently, he signed the contract on the spot, and the property made history in 2004 as the first million-dollar condo sale in the neighborhood, selling for $1.15 million. This record-breaking sale, surpassing the next highest by almost $700,000, marked a significant milestone in the local market.

While some initially deemed our approach unconventional, I trusted in the property's unique appeal and successfully navigated the sale in a few months. It not only closed but also became a benchmark for the neighborhood. This experience highlighted the importance of perseverance, insight, and building lasting connections in the real estate industry.

Michael LaFido:

Tell us about your most memorable luxury transaction and why was it so memorable?

Paul Campano:

I had a single family in a suburb of Boston that was famous or infamous, I'm not sure. It was featured in a couple movies. It was again, another one that was truly off the charts. It was 20,000 square feet.

The gentleman prior had purchased a 10,000 square foot home, completely renovated it and then added on 10,000 square feet, with what I call almost the amenity wing. My favorite feature was this very cool door that went directly from your living room into a full court gymnasium with 40-foot ceilings, and a regulation basketball court. You could play volleyball there, take batting practice or do any number of things in it. Also, there were bleachers for an audience. It also had an indoor two-story water slide into a heated pool, a Tiki bar, bowling alley, home theater, and an English pub. You never had to leave.

It had kind of an interesting history where my clients had owned it for a while and let it sit idle, which was why it was the most infamous property in that area. People had always wondered what was happening with that house. It was a property that had been marketed a few times prior to my taking it on. It was another story of just kind of staying in touch with the sellers. I finally got the opportunity, and we sold it in about five days.

Michael LaFido:

When you see a property with so many cool assets, how can you leverage it? What can you feature through your photos, your videos? I'm sure you were able to leverage the sale after the fact, correct?

Paul Campano:

Absolutely. Crafting a strategy that effectively highlights the unique aspects of a property is truly gratifying. It's crucial to avoid focusing solely on superficial elements when marketing such distinctive properties. While having a cool property is fantastic, it's unrealistic to expect buyers to invest millions solely for its uniqueness. Striking the right balance involves showcasing the property's allure, piquing interest with the 'wow' factors, but also emphasizing the true value it brings. It's about conveying that the property offers more than just visual appeal; it provides tangible and meaningful features that contribute to its overall value.

Michael LaFido:

What are the most important skills and qualities for success in the luxury real estate market as an agent? And how have you developed these skills throughout your career?

Paul Campano:

I think integrity and honesty are things that you can't buy, even though we're talking about luxury homes and very high price sales, these are things that you can't buy, and it can never be bought back should you lose them. I think loyalty, honesty, and integrity are part of that foundation.

I'm not sure that it's exactly a skill, but I think it's developing some type of commonality with the client you want to work with. Sometimes people feel like, well, wait a second, if I'm not already selling multi-million-dollar homes, how do I get into those circles? There are always ways, whether it's going to car shows or educating yourself on private aviation, where you can develop some knowledge around that type of situation. When you can speak their language, it immediately starts to dispel any doubts they may have. You can tell somebody all day long how great you are, all the skills you have, but when you're able to relate to that person and they understand that you do have some commonality and some common interests, that goes a long way.

Michael LaFido:

Let's talk a little bit about technology. It's a big buzzword at all the big conferences and real estate events that I attend. What technology and tools do you utilize to support your work as a luxury real estate agent?

Paul Campano:

In terms of technology, the market is flooded with various products, and the key lies in discerning which ones truly serve the goal rather than getting lost in the allure of the latest trends. I explore emerging technologies to gauge their relevance. For instance, I initially invested in Matterport when it gained popularity, but I now rely on a service for immersive tours, particularly beneficial for engaging international buyers.

While I've experimented with Telepresence—a robot controlled via iPad offering clients a virtual property tour—it's crucial to balance novelty with effectiveness. Despite the constant influx of new tools, I find that traditional methods remain invaluable. Photography plays a significant role. I work with skilled photographers who excel at capturing compositions within the frame. However, recognizing each photographer's strengths, such as composition versus color accuracy, is essential.

For properties with predominantly white or monochromatic furnishings, post-processing becomes crucial. I leverage additional services to enhance photos, ensuring optimal color balance, especially for contemporary-style homes. Moreover, AI-driven filters available in computer-based tools have proven instrumental in highlighting a property's best features. In navigating this tech landscape, the focus remains on utilizing tools that genuinely elevate the property presentation and cater to the specific needs of both buyers and sellers.

Michael LaFido:

Let's talk about innovation. What are you doing to stay ahead of the curve, so to speak?

Paul Campano:

I think it sort of falls back on what we mentioned, always trying to explore. Not being afraid to explore what might be new, whether it's VR goggles or something else. I've done a virtual staging of a property because it was a unique, most expensive condo this city has ever seen, but it was a little dated, believe it or not. What you're able to do is have someone go in and render virtually what a new kitchen would look like, and then you're able to put the goggles on someone and say, okay, maybe you don't have the ability or the vision to see what it could be, but literally, let me show you what that looks like. It's cool that you're able to do that and show people sort of in a 3D environment what that can look like. I've become known for outside of the box marketing...everything from having a local artist spray chalk a for sale sign on a city street, a spoof video that went viral showcasing a client's property for sale to epic VIP open houses for top tier listings.

Michael LaFido:

How do you work with other professionals in the industry such as architects, designers, attorneys, interior designers, you name it, to provide comprehensive services to your clients, whether it be your buyer clients or your out showing properties and your clients want to do some renovations?

Paul Campano:

Absolutely, I completely agree. Maintaining a comprehensive network of allied resources and trusted vendors is incredibly valuable. It goes beyond just having contacts; it's about having reliable professionals like plumbers or electricians who are willing to address smaller issues without the need for a complete rewiring of a property.

Many of my clients often express the difficulty in finding someone for specific tasks. In such cases, I leverage my network, reaching out to trusted individuals who can efficiently handle the job. While tradespeople understandably can't commit to every minor job, these relationships become crucial for quick and reliable solutions.

Furthermore, knowing the crème de la crème in various fields, whether it's interior design, architecture, or any other specialty, serves as an excellent resource. Identifying and maintaining relationships with top-tier professionals is vital. This becomes especially significant when clients acquire high-value properties and plan substantial renovations. Being able to connect them with the right architect to bring their vision to life becomes an invaluable service.

Michael LaFido:

Talk to me about balance. How do you balance providing personalized attention to your clients while managing multiple high net worth clients and maybe buyers or sellers, right? Sometimes they tend to be a little bit more needy, more hands on. How do you balance providing personalized attention to your individual clients while still maintaining multiple clients at the same time?

Paul Campano:

I consider myself fortunate to have a diverse clientele, ranging from traditional buyers and sellers – those seeking single-family homes or selling condos – to a niche market dealing with high-end, distinctive properties and athletes in search of rental or purchase opportunities. Unlike those aiming to sell a large volume of houses annually, I intentionally keep the volume of my business scaled back. This deliberate choice allows me to offer a top-notch service to my clients.

Working with this type of clientele requires a high-touch approach, as their needs are often unique. I prefer to handle things personally rather than outsourcing tasks to assistants or multiple layers of support staff. I maintain a hands-on approach and consciously scale my business to ensure I can consistently provide exceptional services. This way, I never take on more than I can manage, guaranteeing that I can deliver the top-notch service my clients deserve.

Michael LaFido:

Can you describe to me your process for pricing these unique high-end properties? Sometimes they're one of a kind, you mentioned the firehouse earlier. How do you price these high-end luxury properties?

Paul Campano:

This is a question I often receive: "What is your process?" My response is, "It depends." I understand that consumers might think there's a catch or hidden agenda, but I follow up by explaining that my process is tailored to achieve their specific goals. To recommend the best path, I need to understand their objectives. For instance, if there's a need for a quick sale within 30 days, we devise a strategy and game plan geared towards achieving that goal.

On the other hand, if the property is still under construction and there's a six-month runway, we might explore an off-market approach initially. Utilizing my network, we can discreetly introduce the property to potential buyers, assess feedback, and possibly secure an off-market deal at the desired price. If needed, we can later transition to a more traditional exposure strategy. The key is that everything we do is centered around the client's goals and objectives.

We can try to establish what the baseline value is for 60 days on the market. But again, with our clientele, as you know, typically nothing about them tends to be average or traditional. It's really trying to tailor a bespoke approach to their situation and making sure that the game plan that we develop best achieves their desired outcome.

Bonus section

Tips for Home Sellers

Michael LaFido:

When a homeowner is interviewing agents to best market their home, what's the number one tip or suggestion or a few tips and suggestions you have to a homeowner when they're interviewing agents as to what they should look for in an agent to market their home?

Paul Campano:

Experience is undoubtedly a crucial factor. In our market, the presence of hyper-local markets makes it clear that an agent from just five miles away may lack the same knowledge, experience, and crucial relationships with local agents. This local expertise is paramount in maximizing the client's sale and is, in my opinion, the top priority.

Moreover, when dealing with something unique, such as modern and one-of-a-kind properties, having a personal affinity for these types of real estate can be a significant advantage. While not a strict necessity, I believe it adds substantial value to have an agent who genuinely appreciates and connects with the properties they are selling.

Tips for Home Buyers

Michael LaFido:

Flip side of that would be somebody buying a property, whether it's in their primary city, their primary residence, or perhaps a vacation property. What qualities should a buyer look for in an agent to help them decide if they should hire that agent and sign A Buyer Representation Agreement with them?

Paul Campano:

I believe it's crucial to work with someone who aligns with your timeline, especially when seeking something more unique. Such properties often require time and effort to uncover, and the ability to identify opportunities before they hit the market is essential. I can remember a situation where I spotted an owner of a unique building from my database of unconventional places. Despite previous attempts to reach out, he didn't respond. Seizing on the moment, I happened to catch him walking out of this abandoned looking building, expressed my admiration for his building, and asked if he could give me a quick peek inside. During the impromptu tour, we connected, and he revealed a willingness to sell under the right conditions.

This experience underscores the importance of having an agent who not only knows where to look but can also establish meaningful connections, provide exclusive access, and successfully close deals. Having literal "boots on the ground" in my neighborhoods is greatly beneficial for my clients. Whether dealing with unique or traditional homes, having an agent dedicated to working diligently on your behalf is paramount.

Visit: SecretsOfTopLuxuryAgents.com
to learn more about Paul Campano

Connect with Paul Campano by Scanning the QR Code Below

> **"**
> There are three reasons
> homes don't sell:
> 1 – It's overpriced.
> 2- It's underexposed or
> 3- Poorly positioned.
> **"**
>
> Michael LaFido

CHAPTER 21

SANDRA RATHE

From CPA to Real Estate Magnate
A Unique Journey

SANDRA and her team have been top agents in South Florida for the past 14 years, outselling thousands of other agents with their determination, customer service, and top-notch skills. Selling over $138 million in real estate in 2023 alone and nearly a Billion since 2009, gives the team the knowledge and experience needed to best help you with any real estate needs you may have. Sandra and her team rank in the top ½ of 1% of all agents nationwide, earning top awards year after year and earning an elite membership in Keller Williams Luxury, Keller Williams Relocation, and Gary Keller's Top 100 Group.

Sandra began her career with an undergraduate degree in Accounting from George Mason University. Simultaneously, she obtained her Certified Public Accountant's (CPA) license. Directly out of college she began working at Price Waterhouse as a CPA.

Sandra later moved to Illinois to work in corporate accounting and then marketing at Caterpillar. During this time, she earned her MBA graduate degree from Bradley University. Another move brought Sandra to Hartford, Connecticut and United Technologies, where she ultimately became a corporate controller responsible for business entities located throughout the United States and Israel. A final move brought Sandra to sunny South Florida in 2005, where she decided to start her own business in real estate.

Sandra's strong business background makes her a unique real estate professional who not only understands the marketing needs for your home, but also understands the complexities of the numbers, the negotiations and the dedication needed to make your real estate transaction a success.

Sandra has created a team of top agents and extraordinary support staff in order to best serve you and all your real estate needs. Sandra's team has earned numerous honors and awards throughout the years. They have repeatedly been the top team at Keller Williams Legacy and the 5 offices comprising the KW L5L. Additionally, they are the top team in Broward and Miami-Dade and ranked #6 for the entire state of Florida! The team has also achieved the highest honor at Keller Williams by being invited into Gary Keller's inner circle of top 100 Teams. This honor is offered to just the very best agents in the company, ranking in the top 0.1 %. Sandra and her team rank #61 out of over 188,000 agents worldwide at Keller Williams. As a prestigious luxury team and ambassador of luxury, Sandra provides luxury training for both new and experienced agents across the globe with her monthly luxury zoom - Mastering Luxury with Sandra. Sandra also speaks at some of the largest real estate conferences each year, covering topics that include Best Practices for Selling Luxury Real Estate and how to give buyers and sellers the best experience possible throughout the process.

Michael LaFido:

Talk to us about your first luxury sale, and did you represent the buyer or the seller? How did they find out about you and vice versa?

Sandra Rathe:

I obtained my real estate license back in 2009, but it wasn't until the following year, 2010, that I truly began to make strides in the industry. It wasn't long after that, in 2011, when I achieved a significant milestone: my first luxury sale. Prior to this, my typical sales hovered around the $350,000 mark. However, this particular sale shattered that average, ringing in at a remarkable $1,020,000. Needless to say, I was exhilarated by this substantial leap. I first met the clients when they responded to a newsletter I was sending out to my neighborhood where I had built up a considerable portfolio of listings. I represented them in the sale of their house and the purchase of their gorgeous new luxury home. Interestingly, many of the sellers in my neighborhood were transitioning to a more opulent neighborhood, and they entrusted me to guide them through both the selling and buying processes. What made this experience even more enjoyable was that, at the time, the majority of my sales were on the listing side. Thus, to have my first luxury sale come from the buying side was a refreshing change of pace.

Michael LaFido:

If you were to pick one thing that sets you apart from other agents in your local market when it comes to luxury real estate, what would that be and what advice would you have for other agents?

Sandra Rathe:

Absolutely, I'd emphasize knowledge. It's about delving deep into the intricacies of the market, discerning the origins of potential buyers for luxury listings, crafting effective marketing strategies tailored to these properties, and interpreting market signals to determine optimal pricing strategies. Staying ahead in this field requires a keen awareness of shifting trends and anticipating future developments. What worked yesterday may not necessarily work tomorrow, so staying abreast of all trends and preferences is crucial. Essentially, it boils down to maintaining a knowledge-driven approach and continuously educating oneself to remain at the forefront of the industry.

Michael LaFido:

What inspired you to become a luxury real estate agent?

Sandra Rathe:

In my view, breaking into the luxury real estate market isn't just about the occasional stroke of luck or relying solely on connections. It's about elevating your expertise and consistently demonstrating your proficiency. To truly excel in this arena, you must showcase your thorough understanding of the market dynamics and your ability to effectively market high-end properties. Additionally, one must also have a great understanding of the economy, the world of insurance and how it affects a purchase, knowledge of tax consequences of a high value sale, as well as other vehicles for investing. For me, the challenge of meeting these demands was what initially propelled me forward. There is immense satisfaction in assisting high net worth individuals navigate their real estate transactions and facilitate their next move while they are often immersed in philanthropic endeavors, performing demanding jobs or managing large portfolios of investments. Being able to be an integral part of their wealth building, wealth advising and maximizing their personal enjoyment provides me with a very high level of internal satisfaction.

Michael LaFido:

How do you manage clients' expectations to ensure they're fully informed and satisfied with the services? Again, talking about luxury, sometimes I could be a little bit more needy. They are used to a more VIP level of service. How do you manage those expectations?

Sandra Rathe:

This principle holds true across all facets of our work. Whether we're facilitating the sale or purchase of a home, the process is inherently rife with uncertainties and can evoke considerable anxiety. It is crucial to manage clients' expectations by providing clear and consistent communication. When individuals feel uninformed or uncertain about what to expect, it can lead to unnecessary stress and panic. That's why we make it a priority to outline our approach upfront and reinforce it throughout every stage of the transaction.

Moreover, we recognize that people absorb information differently. Some are visual learners, while others prefer auditory cues. To accommodate varying preferences, we ensure that information is disseminated through multiple channels. For instance, while we may discuss details over the phone, we also follow up with a comprehensive email outlining the same points. This multi-faceted approach continues throughout the entire transaction, with both our agents and transaction coordinators providing guidance and clarification. By presenting information in different formats and repeating key details, we aim to ensure that our clients feel informed and supported every step of the way.

Also, we have developed a very detailed system and a repeatable process which helps ensure that every buyer and seller feels well cared for. Being able to communicate that process to our clients gives them a great sense of comfort. We anticipate the challenges and proactively communicate with our clients to prepare them as needed for any potential change in plans.

Lastly, we always have to remember that what seems like a simple step in the process to us, is not always a simple step to the buyer or seller. We must keep in mind that the client doesn't know the process like we do, nor do they know what we are doing behind the scenes unless we tell them. Communicating at a high level is absolutely imperative in order to provide the client with a great experience throughout the process.

Michael LaFido:

Differentiating yourself and your brand in a highly competitive luxury market is critical to success. How do you maintain a strong reputation as well with your referral network to make yourself that differentiator? Also, how do you maintain your reputation, your referral network, and differentiation?

Sandra Rathe:

Let's begin by emphasizing the importance of maintaining a professional image at all times. Whether we're casually shopping at Publix or engaging in any public activity, we must remember that we're constantly in the spotlight. This awareness extends to every aspect of our branding and communication. Whether it's a newsletter, a postcard, or an MLS listing, the quality must always be top-notch. Regardless of the property's value, whether it's a mobile home or a multimillion-dollar mansion, professional-grade photographs and meticulous attention to detail are non-negotiable. Every piece of content we release reflects not just the property, but also our own brand and reputation.

Additionally, cultivating a robust collection of client reviews is paramount. We've garnered over 500 five-star Google reviews and more than 600 five-star Zillow reviews, which serve as powerful endorsements of our services and integrity. Our reviews give future buyers and referral agents a view into what it is like to work with The Sandra Rathe Team. The reviews allow them to get to know us in more detail before they commit to a relationship with us. After reading our reviews they feel much more at ease making the choice to work with us on one of their biggest assets to us.

Furthermore, I make a concerted effort to share my knowledge and expertise with others. Whether it's through teaching sessions on luxury real estate or broader topics within the industry, I'm committed to empowering and educating consumers and fellow professionals. This dedication extends beyond local boundaries; whether I'm in Florida, California, New York, or even Puerto Vallarta, I seize every opportunity to impart knowledge and support others' growth. For instance, I host a monthly Luxury Zoom session open to all, where I not only provide valuable insights but also establish meaningful connections with participants. It's all about giving back and helping others. When people see that you truly do care and want to help, they in turn will trust you with their client referrals or working with you themselves. Real estate is a very personal experience so we must not only show our knowledge and skills, we also must earn other's trust and support.

Michael LaFido:

What technology and tools do you utilize to support your work as a luxury real estate agent, and how do you ensure that you stay ahead of the curve? It seems like every year there's a new buzzword, right? A couple of years ago it was blockchain and then it was ChatGPT, and it maybe still is. What are you doing from a technology standpoint to support your work and what are you doing to stay ahead of the curve?

Sandra Rathe:

There are a couple of important considerations to bear in mind, and one of them is exercising caution when it comes to adopting new technologies. It's tempting to chase after every shiny new gadget or platform that emerges in the real estate sphere, but it's essential to conduct thorough research and evaluation beforehand. Not every innovation is a benefit to our business; some can actually tarnish your professional image or lead to unintended consequences. Therefore, it's crucial to weigh the potential benefits against the risks and consider whether the new technology aligns with your business goals and values.

Continuing education remains paramount. Whether it's tuning in to podcasts, attending real estate seminars nationwide, or participating in events like Keller Williams Mega Camp or Keller Williams Family Reunion, the pursuit of knowledge is perpetual. Personally, I find tremendous value in networking with top performers within

Gary Keller's top 100 teams. Engaging with peers who operate at a similar or higher level allows for invaluable knowledge exchange. By sharing insights on the latest tools and strategies, as well as learning from each other's experiences and failures, we can make informed decisions about which technologies best suit our needs and objectives. By participating in these connections, we learn about the latest technologies at a very early stage, allowing us to take advantage of benefits at a rapid pace. Networking thus, plays a pivotal role in guiding our technological choices.

A few examples of the technologies that we use that help us market homes to the highest level include incorporating the best tools in the photography realm. Not only do we provide great still shots of our homes, we also ensure we have professionally taken aerial photographs and video. For those homes that stand vacant, we may add some warmth to them with virtual staging to give the buyer a better visual understanding of the space. We also may enhance the photos with a few twilight shots to evoke emotions from the buyers which prods them to come see the home.

Aside from photography, we also implement technology to provide our past and potential clients with updated valuations of their homes and of the local market. While this technology is never a replacement for the human analysis that we do, it does provide the consumer with valuable information that can help them determine if they are ready to start the conversation about making a move. With this information our clients can feel connected to us and knowledgeable about the market and again give them a great experience working with us.

Michael LaFido:

What unique qualities or skills do you possess that have helped you succeed? And, if you were to pick up and move to a new state, a new city, your sphere of influence had to start from scratch, what would you do and how would you be successful?

Sandra Rathe:

It goes back to understanding the market and understanding the client. If I were to pick up and move somewhere else, I would spend an extensive amount of time researching the local markets to gain an understanding of pricing, desirability of the different areas, learning the value of various features of the homes and understanding where the buyers for that location generally come from. I was a CPA before I got into real estate, so I understand the importance of research, analysis and understanding the numbers. After hanging up my accounting hat, I moved into the corporate world into a marketing role. I have a unique blend of skill sets that allow me to have an understanding of the numbers and also knowing how to market that information in a way that people can receive it and understand it.

A lot of people don't understand the pricing side, or they understand pricing, but they don't know how to actually market the property. The blend of those two talents and the background that I have with both accounting and marketing, really gives me a big advantage in being able to fully serve my clients at the highest level and ensure that they are well informed and well cared for throughout the process.

Additionally, everything we do on The Sandra Rathe Team has a system and a process, so starting in a new city or area where we don't know anyone would be fairly easy for us. Once we research the market and understand it, we would simply apply the proven systems and processes that we have refined over the last 15 years.

Michael LaFido:

What is your marketing strategy for luxury homes? As you know, these unique properties require a different approach, a specialized approach, and what channels do you use to reach high net worth individuals, buyers, sellers, influencers in the local market as well as outside of that market?

Sandra Rathe:

For us, a significant portion of our luxury properties are sold beyond the borders of Florida. Many affluent individuals from states like New York and California are drawn to our state's allure, particularly due to the absence of income tax and our perpetual sunshine. Understanding the origins of these potential buyers and collaborating with agents in those regions is key. We receive numerous referrals from across the country, but certain areas stand out as particularly fruitful. Therefore, our marketing efforts extend beyond South Florida, encompassing nationwide and global platforms.

During the pandemic, we witnessed a surge in people relocating to Florida from various regions. The relatively lower property prices here compared to other parts of the country make it an attractive destination for many.

Our marketing strategy involves leveraging online platforms such as The Wall Street Journal, Barron's, and Mansions Global, which attract significant activity. Additionally, we feature our homes in luxury magazines distributed nationally, not just locally. While we do flood the local area with print and online marketing, we understand that real estate sales can originate from unexpected sources. Thus, we adopt a comprehensive approach, including targeted Facebook ads tailored to specific regions like California.

We are deliberate in our choice of publications, ensuring they resonate with luxury markets. For instance, advertising in yachting magazines aligns with the lifestyle of many of our clientele, who may also be interested in purchasing yachts. Collaborating with partners whose services complement our clients' needs further enhances our offerings.

We prioritize ensuring that our properties receive maximum exposure. This means employing traditional methods such as professional yard signs, postcards, and newsletters. Additionally, we embrace modern strategies, leveraging the power of social media, online advertising, mastering SEO, rising high on google searches, as well as featuring in luxury magazines. We believe in leaving no stone unturned when it comes to showcasing our listings. Our comprehensive approach encompasses both time-tested techniques and cutting-edge tactics to ensure our clients' homes receive the attention they deserve.

Tips for Home Sellers

Michael LaFido:

What advice would you give to the homeowner that's interviewing agents to sell their luxury home? Whether it's their primary residence, a vacation property, what's one tip or two tips, top couple of tips that you would have that they should consider when hiring an agent to represent them with the sale of their property?

Sandra Rathe:

Absolutely, that's an excellent question. Selling your home can indeed be an emotionally charged process, underscoring the importance of finding the right realtor. Firstly, I would encourage the homeowner to conduct thorough research and compile a shortlist of potential agents. Too often, I've witnessed instances where out-of-area agents list a property and it sells for far below its true value. Homeowners need to exercise savvy judgment by assessing an agent's track record of sales and client satisfaction, particularly within the local market. It's essential to gauge their familiarity with the nuances of the area; after all, selling a home successfully hinges on a deep understanding of its surroundings.

Examining the agent's marketing strategy is paramount. In the luxury segment, there's a misconception that properties sell effortlessly. However, the reality is quite different. Selling luxury real estate demands resilience and a robust marketing budget. It's not merely a matter of listing on the MLS; comprehensive advertising campaigns are necessary. We can delve further into the specifics of this later.

Furthermore, inquiring about past transactions is crucial. Assessing an agent's communication and relationship-building skills is key, as it mirrors how they engage with potential buyers. Ensuring that they listen attentively to your needs is paramount. Negotiation prowess is equally vital, particularly in high-value transactions. It's imperative to understand the agent's approach to negotiations and their track record of securing favorable outcomes for clients.

Additionally, verifying credentials and ensuring the agent's sales history is truly theirs and not their office's is critical. A successful luxury agent should also be able to readily provide a list of their recent sales as well as references and extensive 5 star reviews; any hesitation in this regard raises a red flag for me.

Tips for Home Buyers

Michael LaFido:

Making a shift to somebody buying a property, What qualities should a buyer look for in an agent to help them decide if they should hire that agent and sign A Buyer Representation Agreement with them?

Sandra Rathe:

Sure, a lot of it is the same. On the purchasing side, you want to make sure that that agent is familiar with all the areas that you're going to be looking at. Here in South Florida, sometimes we have people looking in three different counties, so a buyer would want to make sure that the agent is familiar with all of the locations they are interested in and what the areas have to offer.

More importantly, a buyer needs to make sure they are working with an agent who truly understands what the buyer is looking for. Not just what type of house they want, but the type of lifestyle they want to lead. Understanding what is most important to the buyer and why it is important is imperative.

Once you feel you have the right person from a caring, compassionate and understanding of your needs perspective, the next most vital information to understand is what that buyer's agent is going to do for you. There are a lot of buyer's agents out there that are more of a door opener than a true fiduciary. Let's ask, what are you going to do throughout the process that makes you different than any other agent? Where are you actually working hard for me? What does your negotiation strategy look like? When you go into an inspection period, how do you negotiate to ensure I get the best deal and a house that's in great condition? How do you handle the appraisal if the appraisal comes in low? Actually digging into what are the activities that the agent is going to do, how they are going to do them and how those activities will impact your experience is vital.

Visit: SecretsOfTopLuxuryAgents.com
to learn more about **Sandra Rathe:**

Connect with Sandra Rathe by Scanning the QR Code Below

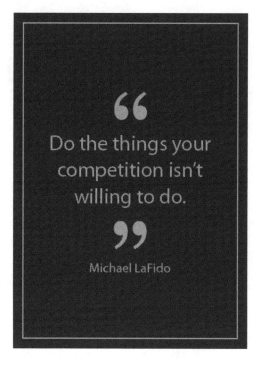

"
Do the things your
competition isn't
willing to do.
"

Michael LaFido

CHAPTER 22

CHRISTOPHE CHOO

Embracing the Luxury Lifestyle to Attract Elite Clients

CHRISTOPHE CHOO is an award-winning, top-producing luxury real estate agent and a Coldwell Banker Global Luxury Ambassador with over 33 years of experience serving Los Angeles' most prominent Westside neighborhoods spanning the Platinum Triangle, including Beverly Hills, Holmby Hills and Bel Air.

Christophe's endless passion and enthusiasm for real estate has earned him a coveted position among the nation's best real estate agents, with more than 500 real estate transactions closed over the course of his career. For many years, he has enjoyed "top producer" status in the Coldwell Banker International President's Premiere, which honors the top 1% of Coldwell Banker agents worldwide. He consistently ranks among the top 100 of Coldwell Banker Global Luxury specialists. He has been ranked among America's top agents in "THE THOUSAND" by REAL Trends as advertised in The Wall Street Journal. His enthusiastic embrace of social media and technology also continues to raise his star status; in 2018, he was voted the No. 1 Real Estate Video Influencer in North America.

Christophe is a frequent guest speaker at organizations and events such as the Asian American Real Estate Association, the Associated Realty of the Americas, Coldwell Banker International Conference, Generation Blue Conference for Coldwell Banker and Your Coach Conferences with Tom Ferry. He has also appeared on several television shows, including HGTV's "Selling LA," Bravo's "Million Dollar Listing," "Beautiful Homes & Great Estates," Luxury Lifestyles TV, Open House TV on NBC, Behind the Gates and "The T.O. Show" on VH1.

Michael LaFido:

Talk to us about your first luxury sale and how did they find out about you and how did you find out about them and were you representing them on the buy side or the sale side?

Christophe Choo:

I believe my first significant luxury sale occurred approximately 25 years ago. It involved a $5.6 million home, which at the time was a substantial milestone for me. Prior to that, my highest sale was around the $2 million mark. Interestingly, this opportunity came to me through a referral from another agent.

I remember attending conferences, as I usually do, and it was at one of these events where I crossed paths with an agent from Honolulu. Upon learning about my expertise in the Beverly Hills and Bel Air areas, he reached out to me. He mentioned that he had a connection with a US Bankruptcy Court trustee who needed representation for a stunning gated property in Bel Air. This property, situated in a gated community, would become one of the highest sale bankruptcy homes in the United States up to that point.

What's remarkable is that this opportunity arose solely from a referral made by an agent I had met at a conference in Hawaii. It underscores the power of networking and the unexpected avenues through which opportunities can arise in the real estate industry.

Michael LaFido:

Reflecting on your remarkable career journey, could you share with us a standout luxury transaction that remains vivid in your memory? What made this particular transaction so memorable for you, and were you representing the buyer or the seller?

Christophe Choo:

One of the most memorable and enjoyable luxury transactions I've had the pleasure of being involved in occurred nearly two decades ago. Close friends of ours reached out to me to list their home, situated in the prestigious Holmby Hills area of Los Angeles. The property, valued at $30 million at the time, boasted stunning architecture and housed an impressive art collection and exquisite antiques.

Initially, the listing presented a challenge as the owners, a husband and wife with three children, were reluctant to properly stage certain rooms for showcasing. Despite this, we embarked on a year-long listing journey. Several months into the process, the owners approached me with a unique proposition – they asked if my family and I would consider residing in the home while it was on the market, as they were relocating abroad.

Though hesitant at first, my wife and I ultimately embraced the opportunity, drawn by the allure of temporarily calling this magnificent 15,000-square-foot mansion our home. We negotiated terms that included an allowance for an orchid and flower budget, as well as permission to restage select rooms using our own collection of French antiques and artwork.

Over the course of nearly eight months, we had the privilege of living in the luxurious estate, hosting exclusive events to showcase the property to potential buyers. One particularly memorable event, a Rolls-Royce party held on the premises, nearly resulted in a sale.

The experience was truly unforgettable – from the sheer opulence of the surroundings to the excitement of promoting such a prestigious property. While bidding farewell to the mansion was bittersweet, knowing that we had successfully facilitated its sale brought a sense of fulfillment.

Leaving behind the lavish amenities, including a spacious walk-in steam shower, to return to our own home was a transition, but one we made with satisfaction, knowing that we had achieved our goal.

Michael LaFido:

Let's dive into the topic of prospecting for luxury clients. Could you share your approach to prospecting for luxury clients and discuss the strategies that have proven successful for you in expanding your network and facilitating easier and more effective prospecting?

Christophe Choo:

When discussing prospecting for luxury clients, it's essential to recognize that traditional methods like calling expired or for sale by owner listings may not apply in the same way. To truly thrive in the luxury market, it's about immersing yourself in that world.

Luxury real estate isn't just a job; it's a lifestyle. To attract luxury clients, you need to live, breathe, and embody the luxury lifestyle. This means being present in their social circles, attending the same events, dining at the same restaurants, and supporting similar causes. By becoming a familiar face in their world, you build trust and credibility, making it more likely for them to choose you when it comes to real estate transactions.

Moreover, expanding your horizons beyond local events and venturing to prominent destinations worldwide can be fruitful. Rubbing elbows with affluent individuals in cities like New York, Paris, or Rome can lead to valuable connections. Rather than immediately discussing real estate, focus on building genuine relationships. Learn about their interests and endeavors, and let the conversation naturally segue into your profession. While they may not need your services immediately, when the time arises, they'll remember you as a trusted and knowledgeable resource.

A prime example of successful prospecting without actively seeking clients is through genuine interactions and maintaining connections. For instance, by regularly attending events hosted by a prestigious jewelry company, my network expanded, leading to meaningful friendships. When the opportunity arose to sell their home, my name was the first to come to mind due to our established rapport.

Ultimately, prospecting in the luxury market is about authenticity, positioning yourself in the right environments, and forming genuine connections with potential clients. By being yourself and seizing opportunities to connect with the right people, you can establish a solid foundation for success in luxury real estate.

Michael LaFido:

How do you keep abreast of market trends, particularly in the realm of luxury real estate? Over the past few years, we've witnessed numerous shifts and fluctuations, from inventory shortages to sudden spikes, along with fluctuations in interest rates, and more. How do you ensure you're up-to-date with these trends, and how do you leverage this knowledge to serve your clients effectively?

Christophe Choo:

I actively participate in a variety of conferences, including prestigious events like the Inman Luxury conferences, as well as Coldwell Banker International Global Luxury conferences, and our regular Coldwell Banker gatherings. Additionally, I've engaged in coaching for the entirety of my 33-year career, receiving guidance from industry leaders such as Tom Ferry and previously, Mike Ferry.

Attending conferences is paramount for staying informed. For instance, next week, I'll be attending an elite retreat in Orlando for top agents within the Tom Ferry ecosystem. These gatherings provide invaluable opportunities to learn from top producers worldwide, gaining insights into winning strategies, effective marketing techniques (ranging from video to social media, internet, and email), and current market trends.

Another essential resource I utilize is Keeping Current Matters, a company founded by Steve Harney. Through their daily emails, I receive pertinent articles curated by their team of 50 employees, covering various aspects of today's real estate landscape tailored for sellers, buyers, and first-time buyers.

Dedicating time to training is crucial. For instance, today, following our discussion, I have a three-hour Zoom conference call with Tom Ferry, focusing on navigating the current market landscape. Additionally, podcasts have become a valuable tool for continuous learning, providing insights during my commute.

By dedicating myself to ongoing education, I ensure that I am well-equipped to serve my clients effectively. When working with buyers or sellers, I can provide informed advice based on current market trends, their individual needs, and their long-term plans. Ultimately, staying informed allows me to act as a trusted advisor, helping clients make well-informed decisions that align with their goals.

Michael LaFido:

In your view, what skills and qualities are paramount for success as a luxury real estate agent, and how have you honed these attributes throughout your career?

Christophe Choo:

When considering the essential skills and qualities for success in the luxury real estate market, expertise in the inventory ranks high.

In areas like the Westside of Los Angeles, where each property is unique, understanding the nuances of the housing stock is crucial. With 33 years of experience under my belt, I make it a priority to attend Broker Caravans every Tuesday. These tours allow me to physically inspect new listings, assessing details like finishes, craftsmanship, views, and neighborhood dynamics firsthand.

My dedication to understanding the inventory was particularly evident when I secured a significant $30 million listing. Despite not having immediate buyers for such high-end properties, I continued to attend Broker Caravans. A colleague questioned the value of this practice, but I understood its importance. By familiarizing myself with luxury properties, I ensured that when the right buyer came along, I would be well-prepared to showcase the most suitable options.

In essence, thorough knowledge of the inventory is foundational in the luxury real estate market. It's not just about knowing what's available; it's about understanding the unique features and characteristics of each property, allowing me to match clients with their ideal homes effectively.

Michael LaFido:

She exhibited negativity towards you, a situation that might have caused some agents to doubt themselves and succumb to her perspective. However, you persevered despite the challenges.

Christophe Choo:

When I received the call for that $30 million listing, my first at that level, I didn't feel nervous at all. I had spent years meticulously studying every home in the area. In those days, I kept detailed notebooks organized by area, filled with brochures from properties I had seen over the years. I was incredibly well-prepared.

One of the top skills for any agent, especially in the luxury market, is the ability to listen attentively to clients and guide them effectively. Clients often have a general idea of what they want, but they rely on agents to provide expert advice and direction, much like consulting a doctor or attorney. While clients may not always agree with the guidance given, they typically trust the expertise of their agent and follow their advice for optimal results.

So, it's essential to possess not only knowledge but also the skill to listen and advise accordingly. It's a multifaceted approach, and honing these skills comes with ongoing education and experience.

Michael LaFido:

My next question is about your approach to collaborating with professionals in the real estate industry, both directly and indirectly. Directly related professionals might include architects, designers, stagers, and attorneys, while indirectly related individuals could be CPAs, financial advisors, and others. Can you share insights into how you've expanded your network of influential contacts in the area who can refer business to you, and vice versa?

Christophe Choo:

I believe referrals stem from the trust you build by consistently providing exceptional service and connecting clients with the right professionals. As a luxury agent, you're not just selling homes; you're offering a comprehensive lifestyle concierge service. Many luxury buyers have multiple properties worldwide, and when they're seeking a home in a new location like Los Angeles, they often require assistance beyond real estate.

For instance, I recently assisted clients from Poland in purchasing a $7 million property that needed renovation. To transform their backyard into a luxurious retreat, I connected them with a top landscape architect renowned for crafting stunning pools and outdoor spaces. Additionally, I facilitated introductions to experts in security systems, home theaters, staging, painting, and maintenance.

Maintaining a trusted network of skilled professionals is vital. Clients rely on these resources, and any missteps reflect poorly on me. By ensuring that each referral delivers exceptional results, I not only enhance client satisfaction but also foster long-term relationships and generate further business opportunities.

Ultimately, it's about providing value beyond the transaction, anticipating clients' needs, and delivering exceptional service at every turn. This approach not only builds trust and loyalty but also encourages referrals and strengthens the reputation of both myself and my network of professionals.

Michael LaFido:

What's your approach to marketing luxury homes? Given their uniqueness and the smaller pool of qualified buyers, how do you ensure your listings stand out and attract attention? Could you elaborate on the strategies you employ to reach high-net-worth potential buyers and sellers, and which channels do you find most effective for this purpose?

Christophe Choo:

Each luxury home presents a unique marketing challenge, requiring a tailored approach to reach potential buyers effectively. When listing a property, I analyze the potential buyer profile. Is it a local buyer, a snowbird seeking a warm escape, or an international buyer from Europe or Asia? This understanding helps me craft targeted marketing strategies.

While local buyers make up the majority, international buyers also play a significant role. I leverage my sphere of influence by proactively reaching out to acquaintances and informing them about new listings. By demonstrating a commitment to their interests, even when the property may not suit them personally, I reinforce the idea that I will advocate for them when they decide to buy or sell.

Collaborating with other agents is another vital aspect of my marketing strategy. Whether it's inviting them to private preview events or directly contacting agents who may have potential buyers, building professional relationships within the industry is invaluable.

In terms of marketing channels, YouTube has been a standout platform for showcasing luxury properties. Additionally, ensuring visibility on Google search results for relevant keywords attracts potential buyers who may not be familiar with me personally but are actively searching for properties in specific areas.

Maintaining a strong presence on social media is essential. Inspired by Gary Vaynerchuk's advice to be a content "DJ" and "mayor" of the community, I produce diverse content about the lifestyle and amenities of the areas I serve. By sharing insights about restaurants, events, and local attractions, I provide valuable information to potential buyers unfamiliar with the area, positioning myself as a knowledgeable guide.

Through consistent content creation across various social media platforms, I've established connections with agents and clients, leading to significant referral business. By staying active on platforms like LinkedIn, Instagram, and Facebook, I ensure that my network remains engaged and informed.

An amusing anecdote underscores the power of social media in generating referrals. A $10 million listing referral from Bel Air came about because of a video I shared during a home inspection. It's a testament to the impact of authentic, relatable content in fostering connections and driving business growth.

Bonus Section

Tips for Home Sellers

Michael LaFido:

The initial question is directed at homeowners contemplating selling their high-end and distinctive properties, who may be unsure about what criteria to consider or questions to pose when selecting an agent. As you're aware, not all agents possess the same expertise, particularly in the realms of luxury real estate, marketing strategies, database management, sphere of influence, and creativity.

What's your foremost advice and guidance for homeowners of upscale and distinctive properties, whether it's their primary residence or vacation home, as they evaluate agents during the interview process? What key attributes or qualifications should they prioritize when seeking the right agent to represent their property?

Christophe Choo:

First and foremost, seek out an agent with whom you can genuinely connect because you're embarking on a relationship that may last anywhere from a month to several years, particularly in the luxury market where properties can take time to sell due to their unique characteristics and limited buyer pool. It's crucial that your agent excels in communication, promptly addressing your needs and providing clear explanations of the selling process, especially if you're unfamiliar with it.

For instance, I recently listed a $3.6 million property for clients who had never sold real estate in the United States before. They had simple yet significant questions that underscored the importance of having an agent who can patiently guide you through every step.

Confidence in your agent is paramount. Ensure they are committed to investing the necessary time, money, and effort into marketing your property effectively. This includes utilizing video marketing, social media promotion, and creating high-quality collateral materials to showcase your home in the best possible light.

Honesty is also essential. Some agents may inflate listing prices or offer reduced commissions to entice sellers, but it's crucial to work with someone who provides a realistic assessment of your property's value. I always prioritize honesty and transparency with my clients, offering realistic pricing strategies and outlining clear plans for achieving their goals.

Lastly, choose an agent with a strong work ethic who is fully dedicated to their craft. Part-time agents may lack the availability and commitment needed to navigate the complexities of the luxury real estate market effectively. You want someone who is fully immersed in the industry and has a proven track record of success.

Tips for Home Buyers

Michael LaFido:

On the flip side, for buyers seeking either their primary residence or a vacation property, What qualities should a buyer look for in an agent to help them decide if they should hire that agent and sign A Buyer Representation Agreement with them?

Christophe Choo:

You'll want to seek out an agent who possesses a deep understanding of the local area and is well-connected within the brokerage community. In the high-end market, where a significant portion of sales occur off-market, these connections are invaluable. Without strong ties to other top agents, you may miss out on private previews or off-market listings. Similarly, as an agent representing buyers, I actively engage with fellow brokers to uncover upcoming listings or off-market opportunities that match my clients' criteria. It's crucial to work with an agent who is not only knowledgeable and connected but also honest and transparent. As with selling agents, integrity is paramount in the buying process. Furthermore, success in luxury real estate requires a considerable amount of effort and dedication. Finding the right property often involves more than just searching the MLS; it requires proactive networking and involvement in private discussions and events.

For instance, I'm currently exploring a potential off-market opportunity for a client interested in a specific area. By leveraging my network and personal connections, I've identified a property that aligns perfectly with their needs. This kind of instinct and networking can lead to successful transactions that may not have been possible through traditional channels alone. Ultimately, the breadth of one's connections and the ability to capitalize on them greatly enhances the chances of finding the perfect property or assisting a seller in achieving their goals.

Visit: SecretsOfTopLuxuryAgents.com
to learn more about Christophe Choo

Connect with Christophe Choo by Scanning the QR Code Below

CHAPTER 23

KOFI NARTEY

*Beyond the Transaction, Building a Global Network
in Luxury Real Estate*

Aleading authority on luxury real estate, Kofi Nartey is the go-to broker for affluent clientele, celebrities, and prominent sports figures around the globe. The CEO of GLOBL RED Real Estate and Development (a REAL Broker partner), a private real estate firm with billions of dollars in sales, Kofi has over 20 years of experience representing elite buyers and sellers of distinguished properties. He regularly appears on national stages, on television and in print media outlets as an industry expert. He was also a featured agent on HGTV's "Selling LA" and has made numerous appearances on "Million Dollar Listing" and "Selling Sunset."

Trusted and admired for his integrity, discretion, and insider knowledge, Kofi is sought out by discerning individuals, professional athletes, and entertainment figures looking for a high level of access and expertise. Prior to GLOBL RED, Kofi was the founder and national director of the Compass Sports & Entertainment Division, where he created and led the nation's first true group of vetted sport and entertainment specialists for four years. He previously served as the director of the Sports and Entertainment Division for the boutique firm The Agency and was a top producer for Keller Williams. Kofi's experience with both boutique and national real estate firms has helped him achieve the perfect balance of bespoke client services, cutting-edge technology, and global real estate reach.

Kofi continues to give to the industry through his speaking, coaching and the "Full Mogul Podcast." He and his wife Mimi also give back through their family foundation, The Nartey Sports Foundation

Michael LaFido:

Tell me about your first luxury sale. Did you represent the buyer or the seller and how did you get that opportunity to work with them?

Kofi Nartey:

My first luxury sale was a house in the strand section of Manhattan Beach, CA. It was my first multi-million dollar listing, and it came almost nine months after launching my "luxury brand." It took that long to get my first opportunity, but there was no looking back after that. The client came through my personal sphere, but it took redefining myself as a luxury agent to give them the confidence to work with me. I invested lots of time and energy into the marketing of that property. I was able to use those high-quality photos on my website and in my marketing materials for years after selling that house.

Michael LaFido:

What was your most memorable luxury transaction and why? (buy or list side)

Kofi Nartey:

My most memorable luxury transaction was a property that didn't sell, but led to $5 million dollars in sales over the following six months. I had a $2.6M celebrity listing. Another celebrity came to see it. They didn't buy that house, but appreciated my expertise and professionalism during the showing, and asked if I could assist them. It turned out that they needed help selling their home and finding a new home. I ultimately sold their house for $1.7M and found them a new home for $3.3M. My original listing never sold because my original client decided not to move, but look what being prepared led to.

This reminded me that our business is not always linear. You won't always see direct results from your specific inputs, but your continued efforts prepare you for what may be next. This keeps you positioned and ready for the opportunities when they show up.

Michael LaFido:

What inspired you to become a luxury Realtor, and what sets you apart from other agents in the market?

Kofi Nartey:

I wanted to utilize my experience, gifts, and talents to service a segment of the industry that I had worked with and knew needed specialized services. I started my career with a focus on condos and townhomes because I owned a townhome and was the HOA president. This is what I knew and built my early business on. Once

I decided to level up my price points, I did research on the clientele and areas I wanted to service. I knew it would be important for me to understand them better than any other agent in the market. I paired this with my prior experience as a professional athlete and actor and started building my expertise and position as a go to broker for celebrity and luxury real estate.

Michael LaFido:

What are the most important skills and qualities for success in the luxury real estate market, and how have you developed these skills throughout your career?

Kofi Nartey:

The important skills for success in luxury real estate are similar to the important skills for success at a high level for anything in life. You must be committed to excellence! You must know your market, your contracts, your statistics, and understand your clientele better than anyone else. There will always be more to learn and ways to get better, so you must always be in search of ways to make each aspect of your business and service better. Excellence is an iterative process.

Michael LaFido:

How do you work with other professionals in the industry, such as architects, designers, and attorneys, to provide comprehensive services to your clients?

Kofi Nartey:

My team has always worked closely with other industry professionals. 'Who you know' matters in luxury real estate. Having the right connections and resources to better service your clients can make you invaluable to your clients. It is also important to bring value to the other industry professionals you work with. Send them referrals. Make strategic introductions for them. Send them articles or events that are relevant to their business. It is also important to share best practices with each other as they relate to your shared clientele. I love bringing an interdisciplinary approach to my business. There is much to learn from other professionals you can work with.

Michael LaFido:

Can you describe your process for pricing luxury properties?

Kofi Nartey:

Pricing luxury properties is part science and part art. Most luxury homes are unique and don't fall neatly into your average comparable analysis. The goal is to capture the value of the home through its story and to be able to justify that value through market knowledge and statistics. Ideally, we can price the home to capture all the value the market will bear without overpricing it. Sometimes we see "aspirational pricing," that functions as a marketing tool to make the property stand out as a trophy asset. We saw this with the Playboy Mansion in the Los Angeles market. It was originally listed for $200M and sold for $100M.

Ultimately, we want to start with a price the research can support, and the story can enhance. The market will ultimately dictate the final price, with a little boost from us experienced agents.

Michael LaFido:

What unique qualities or skills do you possess that have helped you succeed as a luxury realtor?

Kofi Nartey:

One thing that has been key to my success is a commitment to collaboration. This stems from my experience playing team sports. There is an African proverb that says, "If you want to go fast, go alone. If you want to go far, go together." At this stage of my career, I am fully committed to going far and helping others around me go far too. There is much to gain from collaboration with the right people. It gives you the opportunity to share from your gifts and pour into them, as well as benefit from the synergies and leverage of partnership. This is part of the reason I created my coaching program and podcast. It allows me to share my experience by helping agents around the country with their luxury listing opportunities.

Bonus Section

Tips for Home Sellers

Michael LaFido:

What are a few tips and recommendations for owners of a luxury home who are interviewing Realtors to sell their home?

Kofi Nartey:

There are a few things that sellers should look for when interviewing agents. Experience, reach and a system. The agent should have experience selling properties at that price point (or have a partner who does). There are nuances to selling luxury homes in specific areas that experienced agents have learned over time. They must know how to sell the lifestyle of the area.

Reach and the ability to expose the property to the right buyers is important. It took me the better part of five years to build my national and international database of affluent clientele. Now I can use that database to sell luxury homes around the country and new developments around the world.

The third thing sellers should look for is a specific system to sell their property. A system allows the seller to know what to expect and helps take the stress out of the process. We have our A.C.E. Marketing process that is one part of our three-part system. Each letter stands for something and informs the client on what to expect from our process and expertise.

Tips for Home Buyers

Michael LaFido:

When interviewing Realtors to help a buyer find their dream luxury home, what qualities should a buyer look for in an agent to help them decide if they should hire that agent and sign A Buyer Representation Agreement with them?

Kofi Nartey:

When buyers are interviewing agents to find their home, they should look for experience, negotiating ability, and service. The agent should know the market and know the contracts. This will help protect the buyers' interests through the process. Buyers are being guided through the process and they need to feel like they are in great hands.

Negotiating ability is also important for buyers to consider when selecting an agent. Every buyer wants to get the best deal, but the best deal isn't just about price. It is also about terms, timelines, and temperaments. Agents often have to manage life-changing transitions and all of the challenges that are a part of that. Negotiating ability helps make the transition easier.

Service throughout the process is also a key ingredient in selecting an agent. Simple things like responsiveness and resourcefulness are critical to ensuring a smooth transaction. Buyers agents should have vendors and resources that can help the client through every aspect of the buying and moving process.

Visit: SecretsOfTopLuxuryAgents.com
to learn more about Kofi Nartey

Connect with Kofi Nartey by Scanning the QR Code Below

66

The most listened to radio station that your clients and prospects listen to is WIIFM, which stands for "What's In It For Me?" What are you going to do to save your clients and prospects time, aggravation and money?

99

Michael LaFido

PART 2

RISING STARS

CHAPTER 24

TANYA CHAMBERS

Embracing the Luxury Market
A Journey of Growth and Strategy

TANYA CHAMBERS possesses an in-depth understanding of the local market trends, property values, and neighborhoods in Fredericksburg and the surrounding Texas hill country. Whether clients are looking to buy their dream home or sell their property for the best possible price, Tanya is well-equipped to guide them through the entire real estate process. She offers valuable advice, conducts thorough market research, negotiates skillfully, and ensures a smooth and successful transaction for her clients. Trust in her to always have your best interests at heart and put you, as her client, first in every transaction. The surrounding agents know her reputation to negotiate for her clients. She will represent your listing professionally and will always bring you a buyer at the advertised asking price with few exceptions. She's a mother,step mother, grandmother and a previous 2 sport college scholarship athlete that represents her clients with true skill and professionalism rarely seen in the real estate industry.

Michael LaFido:

Did you have specific aspirations when entering the luxury real estate sector?

Tanya Chambers:

After obtaining my real estate license,I opened my own real estate office in the small west texas town of Alpine Texas. My partner and I started from scratch and with-in a year had 40+ ongoing listings. Five years later I relocated to a town poised to become a lucrative luxury market. Growing up elsewhere, I was unfamiliar with the area and didn't have any connections. My objective from the outset was to establish my brand as a luxury agent, even though, at the time, many questioned what that designation meant. Back then, most agents didn't differentiate themselves in such a way; they were simply referred to as Realtors. I was determined not to be just another agent and avoided the risk of blending in with those who pursued real estate part-time.Many of my fellow agents thought it to be funny that I designated myself as a luxury agent at the time and made fun of me for doing so.

My new home is Fredericksburg Texas, a small Texas town of 10,000 people and approximately 678 MLS agents. The average price point is $700,000, contributing to an annual volume of approximately $200 billion. Those are some relatively large numbers, for a town of this size. My primary goal was to position myself for success and stand out amid the crowded real estate landscape, ensuring that I didn't become just another realtor. Blending in was not an option.

Michael LaFido:

What has been the most challenging aspect for you in entering the luxury real estate market?

Tanya Chambers:

Becoming the town's go-to real estate authority is crucial, ensuring that everyone recognizes you and associates you as the foremost expert. In small towns, much like many others, everyone seems to know a Realtor, and familial or community connections play a significant role. One might think that a client would insist on doing business with their relatives or acquaintances, but when it comes to their most lucrative asset, they turn to someone they trust to know the market, who will secure the highest price, and expedite the transaction seamlessly.The challenge is to continually market yourself in your community and be everywhere doing community service and supporting the local landscape while still being human, approachable, and loving to everyone.

Despite concerns about potential conflicts of interest, consistently proving your expertise and becoming the trusted figure in the community is paramount. Repeatedly demonstrating your knowledge of the market and actively engaging with the community to position yourself as the "mayor" of your town. It's a matter of being not just a Realtor, but the reliable authority that people turn to when dealing with their most significant transactions.

Michael LaFido:

What was the primary limiting belief that you had to overcome personally to enter the luxury real estate market?

Tanya Chambers:

The belief I had to overcome was that I hadn't achieved a billion dollars in sales the previous year, questioning whether I could truly consider myself a luxury realtor. I pondered what specific threshold would define me as a luxury realtor compared to others engaged in potentially higher-dollar sales or greater transaction volumes. Eventually, I adopted the mindset that it's not solely about the quantity but the exceptional quality I deliver.

I focused on representing each listing with sterling quality, aligning with the name of our real estate company, Sterling. Emphasizing quality and ethical practices, even if I had just one listing at a time, became my priority. I firmly believed that by consistently delivering excellence, one listing would lead to another, creating a positive momentum. The key was to take that initial step and simply START.

Michael LaFido:

What advice would you offer to an agent who hasn't yet experienced selling luxury homes but is keen to attract luxury buyers and sellers to their client base?

Tanya Chambers:

I suggest that they identify someone in their market who excels in luxury real estate and model their approach. If there's no such person in their immediate market, seeking inspiration from someone in a neighboring market who aligns with their desired approach is a viable strategy. While it may feel akin to a form of observation, the key is to learn from someone already succeeding in the way you aspire to.

Emulating their methods and conducting business in a similar fashion is acceptable, and, in many cases, reaching out to them directly would be beneficial. Expressing a sincere intention to follow their lead and replicate their successful practices is generally well-received. Most individuals in such a position would appreciate the acknowledgment and your willingness to learn. Initiating contact with a message like, "I'm aiming to model my business after yours because you're doing it the way I aspire to. Would you be open to sharing some insights?" often leads to a positive response, as many are willing to share their knowledge when approached with respect and a genuine desire for guidance and mentorship.

Michael LaFido:

How do you approach marketing high-end and luxury homes, and what specific aspect of your strategy sets you apart from local competitors?

Tanya Chambers:

I previously worked for a Fox Television affiliate in Boise Idaho, specializing in marketing, and creating commercials for high-end car dealers and jewelry stores. Upon moving to Texas and obtaining my real estate license, I recognized that my background in marketing was a unique asset that set me apart from many others in the field. My focus lies in employing strategies inspired by successful approaches, such as those found in your playbook.

I emphasize creating emotional connections in my advertising and property presentations. Instead of relying solely on static images, I leverage commercials, videos, and platforms like YouTube to showcase the emotions associated with living in a particular property. By portraying the experiences and feelings one can expect, I aim to stand out in a landscape where others may rely on more traditional methods, ultimately garnering attention even in a seemingly static market.

Michael LaFido:

How has obtaining and hosting the LUXE Designation influenced your ability to overcome objections from buyers or sellers and differentiate yourself in the local market as an agent?

Tanya Chambers:

Once again, the LUXE Designation provided me with the confidence to execute effective marketing strategies without hesitation. It empowered me to engage in video creation, employ models, and go above and beyond what others were doing in the local market. Witnessing the success of these methods across various sales price points, including higher ones than my current focus, reassured me that the approach would work. Embracing the belief that it's acceptable to stand out a bit and be different, I implemented these strategies with the conviction that they would yield positive results.

Interestingly, I first encountered your expertise Michael in Boca Raton during my time with Keller Williams Luxury. Your impactful presentation left an impression. I retained some of your screenshots and slides that I still use in my listing presentations. Our paths crossed again in 2021 at a real estate conference in Las Vegas where we derived a plan to work together the following year. You and your team brought the LUXE Designation to Fredericksburg in 2022! You dropped more marketing nuggets, and as always, your insights provided me with a valuable edge over the competition. In the following years I have won many $1.5M+ property listings over my competition.

Michael LaFido:

We've recently introduced a formal coaching program called LUXE Coaching. For those contemplating LUXE Coaching, what guidance would you offer? You've been familiar with my work since your Keller Williams days, from hosting a LUXE Designation training to our various free training initiatives, podcast, blog, and this book. What advice do you have for individuals considering an investment in LUXE Coaching?

Tanya Chambers:

If you have the means to engage a luxury coach, it's a clear choice—go for it!

Affordability is paramount, and if there's any doubt, consider the intricacies because success often lies in the details. Every year, being inspired by individuals like you, Elena, and others featured in this book, I'm reminded that sticking to the old ways in real estate is not an option. To avoid reverting to ordinary practices, it's crucial to consistently have a coach, mentor, or some form of guidance to aspire towards continual improvement. Without this commitment, there's a risk of falling back into the routine ways of our market peers, hindering our ability to achieve the goals we've set. Failure is not an option for me, and that's why I continually seek to surround myself with mentors like you, offering classes to uplift my agents and ensuring we always strive for greatness.

Bonus Section

Tips for Home Sellers

Michael LaFido:

What tips or advice would you offer homeowners with unique properties when interviewing agents? Can you provide a few tips for sellers to consider when selecting an agent to represent the sale of their home?

Tanya Chambers:

For sellers, it's crucial to seek out a savvy negotiator. This skill isn't universal among agents and may not be present in your family members or part-time agents from your community. A shrewd negotiator is someone who prioritizes your interests, diligently advocates on your behalf, and is adept at navigating challenges inherent in high-end negotiations. Choosing an agent with these negotiation skills ensures they can secure the optimal deal for you.

Michael LaFido:

Securing the best negotiation on their behalf—is there anything else significant, or is that the primary focus?

Tanya Chambers:

It is crucial to find a Realtor who will relentlessly pursue what is best for you. As I mentioned, it's not the Realtor you know from "church." In a competitive market like this, when you find a property you truly desire, you need someone who will actively work to secure the asset without hesitation.

Ensuring that you don't lose money in negotiations is paramount, especially during inspections and other phases. Often, individuals end up losing money unknowingly because their agent wasn't assertive enough to go after what was necessary and they make unnecessary concessions on your behalf.

Tips for Home Buyers

Michael LaFido:

If I'm a consumer exploring a purchase of a home, either abroad or within the US, and I'm interviewing agents to find the best representation for myself and my family, particularly to secure the best home, what qualities should a buyer look for in an agent to help them decide if they should hire that agent and sign A Buyer Representation Agreement with them?

Tanya Chambers:

A crucial factor is finding a specialist, particularly one specialized in the exact area and location you're interested in for buying or investing. This specialist not only excels as a shrewd negotiator but is also a local agent with extensive knowledge and experience in high-end luxury or investment properties within your target area. Their established professional network within the community is invaluable, ensuring a smooth transition for the buyer. Partnering with an agent lacking these connections can result in a prolonged and challenging transaction. As a connected Realtor with agents on my team all over the world I can help you find such an agent to help you with your transaction anywhere in the world. Having a valuable teammate and Raltor on your side is imperative if you are a first time buyer or a lucrative investor. Connections across state borders, international borders and agency borders are imperative in finding that one of a kind property for my clients.

Visit: SecretsOfTopLuxuryAgents.com
to learn more about Tanya Chambers

Connect with Tanya Chambers by Scanning the QR Code Below

CHAPTER 25

CORY TALASKA

Breaking Into Luxury Real Estate
A Personal Journey

CORY TALASKA boasts a seasoned real estate career spanning back to 2014. Her expertise lies in serving both sellers and buyers, and she possesses a profound understanding of the intricate dynamics within the real estate market. Drawing from her background in the critical environment of the operating room, Cory excels in attention to detail, multitasking, and executing tasks with precision and efficiency. In today's fiercely competitive market, Cory leverages her unwavering commitment to continuous learning and personal growth, propelling her to new heights in the luxury real estate sector. Her area of focus includes assisting buyers and sellers in Wisconsin and Florida.

Cory shines brightly within our real estate community, embodying the future of luxury real estate. This section of the book is dedicated to agents poised on the brink of entering the exclusive luxury market. The book's overarching goal is to spotlight individuals like Cory who exemplify relatability, in contrast to the typical portrayal of billionaire agents often magnified by the media. Cory's wealth of experience and insightful guidance serves as an inspirational beacon for those aspiring to excel in the realm of luxury real estate.

Michael LaFido:

What did you hope to achieve by entering the luxury real estate market?

Cory Talaska:

I want to express my gratitude for featuring me in the Rising Stars section of this book. It's a privilege to have the opportunity to impart my knowledge to budding agents.

Venturing into the luxury real estate market is a shared aspiration among many in our industry. Initially, it may seem like a distant dream, particularly in a smaller market like Milwaukee, WI. The challenge is significant, but I'm steadily making headway, thanks to the exceptional training I've received. The magnificent homes along Lake Drive have always captivated me – those homes I've driven past and admired my entire life. My dream extends beyond merely selling them; it's about comprehending every intricate detail that makes them so enticing. I aim to grasp the very essence of these properties, understand what it takes to market such exquisite residences, and collaborate closely with clients who have a profound appreciation for life's finer things.

For me, this journey is not just about a career; it's a way of life. I envision it as a lifestyle I want to fully embrace, with the goal of residing in one of those luxury homes myself someday. I'm brimming with excitement for the path ahead, and I am resolute in my determination to transform that dream into a reality.

Michael LaFido:

What was the number one limiting belief that you had to overcome to break into luxury real estate?

Cory Talaska:

In the early stages, my progress was hindered by my limited experience. Recognizing the need for a shift in my mindset, I had to release the belief that my lack of experience would forever impede my advancement.

My journey is defined by a perpetual commitment to learning and personal growth, serving as my driving force. Whenever I encounter challenges or opportunities to list a luxury property, I prioritize seeking solutions. For instance, if I find myself working with an unrealistic seller, I know that you are just a phone call away and always willing to provide your invaluable assistance. Your recent guidance, when I presented a scenario and sought answers, reaffirmed that I was on the right path, reinforcing the importance of reaching out for support when needed.

Michael LaFido:

What advice would you offer to an agent who has not yet experienced selling luxury homes but aspires to include high-end buyers or sellers in their clientele?

Cory Talaska:

My most invaluable advice is to maintain unwavering perseverance, especially when confronted with challenges. Each obstacle you encounter serves as a valuable lesson, molding both your life and your career. The real estate industry, with its dynamic nature, can often feel like a roller coaster ride, and it's vital to embrace a mindset of continuous learning and growth.

While staying within your comfort zone may be enticing, it can ultimately lead to stagnation. To break into the luxury market, prioritizing self-investment becomes paramount. Surround yourself with mentors and knowledge resources, even if it requires an investment of time and resources. The insights you gain will prove to be invaluable; much of my expertise and success can be attributed to the training and mentorship I've actively pursued.

Michael LaFido:

To help differentiate yourself from other agents, help you increase your average sales price and break into luxury real estate, you invest in the Luxury Listing Specialist Designation (LUXE). How have you leveraged the LUXE Designation?

Cory Talaska:

I've recently adopted the LUXE branding, a choice I'm genuinely enthusiastic about. This branding is now an integral part of my comprehensive business rebranding. It underscores the undeniable importance of self-investment.

The significance of acquiring knowledge and refining one's skills cannot be emphasized enough in the pursuit of professional growth. Merely treading the familiar path and remaining stationary is insufficient. Genuine progress necessitates a proactive stance toward continuous learning and development.

For a full decade, my specialization revolved around selling standard residential, single-family homes. I had comfortably maneuvered within that realm. However, recognizing the imperative need for both personal and professional growth, I found it crucial to step out of my comfort zone. This realization prompted me to embark on a voyage of self-improvement and higher education, which I consider indispensable for enhancing my proficiency and embracing the intricacies of a more intricate and competitive market. My unwavering commitment to ongoing education fuels my pursuit of attaining a higher echelon of expertise in the realm of real estate.

Michael LaFido:

It seems like you've broadened your resource pool, and if you encounter a question without an immediate answer, you know the right avenues to explore. Can we say that your confidence has grown to go after opportunities (listings or buyers) in geographical areas where you haven't yet made a sale because of what you have learned from LUXE?

Cory Talaska:

I've come to appreciate the invaluable support network available to me. There are many individuals, like yourself, as well as those I've had the privilege to learn from, who are just a phone call away whenever I need to discuss or navigate a particular situation. It's reassuring to know that I can always ask, "What's the best approach when dealing with this type of seller or buyer?"

Obtaining the LUXE Designation has played a significant role in my professional growth. It's not just about being certified in luxury itself; it's necessary to have a mentor right at your side, ready to assist whenever I require guidance or a confidence boost. I consider this aspect to be immensely valuable and believe that it justifies every part of the investment in becoming LUXE Certified.

Bonus Section

Tips for Home Sellers

Michael LaFido:

What recommendations do you have for a high-end home seller with an upper price point property who may not have sold a home in some time when they are in the process of interviewing potential agents?

Cory Talaska:

Establishing a genuine connection with the chosen agent is crucial because some individuals tend to tell potential clients what they want to hear. I recommend that sellers conduct interviews with multiple agents to thoroughly assess their marketing strategies and whether they have a pool of prospective luxury property buyers.

Furthermore, it's essential to ensure a strong rapport with the selected agent and have the confidence that they are truly committed to selling your home. The emphasis should be on their dedication to the task at hand rather than simply telling you what you want to hear to secure the listing, only to fall short on fulfilling their responsibilities.

Tips for Home Buyers

Michael LaFido:

What qualities should a buyer look for in an agent to help them decide if they should hire that agent and sign A Buyer Representation Agreement with them?

Cory Talaska:

When it comes to representing buyers, having an agent who possesses a deep understanding of the area is paramount. For instance, even if I haven't personally sold homes in Lake Geneva, I would go the extra mile to familiarize myself with every aspect of that locale. I'd delve into thorough research and self-education to ensure that I can confidently provide answers to any questions my clients may have about the area.

Visit: SecretsOfTopLuxuryAgents.com
to learn more about Cory Talaska

Connect with Cory Talaska by Scanning the QR Code Below

CHAPTER 26

LUCINDA GADSON

From First Sale to Market Mastery
A Realtor's Journey

LUCINDA specializes in high-end and luxury homes across North Texas and she is renowned for her collaboration with builders and adept selling of clients' homes. She is a skilled negotiator, securing adequate lease backs until clients have the keys to their new homes. Additionally, Lucinda assists in finding down payment assistance and negotiating to help with closing costs. Clients' needs are truly heard and covered through their intuitive approach, ensuring a personalized experience. Consistently ranking among Texas' top 500 realtors, she brings over a decade of experience. Her wealth of experience is dedicated to enhancing clients' real estate journeys with unparalleled expertise.

Lucinda increased her average sales price by 60% since attending Michael LaFido's LUXE Designation training in Dallas.

Michael LaFido:

What were your aspirations as an agent when you decided to venture into the luxury real estate market?

Lucinda Gadson:

Living in my neighborhood, it's tough seeing other agents' signs pop up all the time. I wanted to specialize in high-end homes to better serve my community and surroundings. As I delved into it, I found the effort pays off more significantly. Not only financially but also in terms of client appreciation. It's a win-win situation.

Michael LaFido:

What was the toughest part for you getting into or breaking into the luxury real estate market?

Lucinda Gadson:

The toughest part of getting into the high-end homes or the luxury market is delegating the small stuff. I had told you, Michael, that I just moved and I'm trying to saturate the area just to be able to get my name out and I did it again. It is the hardest part. You take a starter home and then you don't have time to go out and market in the areas to get a luxury listing, to get a luxury buyer because you're over in the other neighborhood. If you delegate that to another agent, to someone on your team, then you have time to get your marketing. You only have 24 hours in your day, so it's wise to choose your highest and best use of your time.

Michael LaFido:

What was the number one limiting belief that you had to overcome as an agent to break into luxury real estate? I call them limiting beliefs. Sometimes people call them excuses. We all have them, but what was your number one limiting belief that you had to break into luxury?

Lucinda Gadson:

I used to feel like I had to emulate others' lavish gestures to be successful. Take one of my clients, for example; she gifted Porsches to her entire family last Christmas, including her son-in-law and grandkids. While I can't match that, I felt pressured to mirror her lifestyle before I felt worthy of selling her more properties. But then I realized something profound. I work hard for what I have. For instance, when I needed a new Volvo, instead of waiting for an emergency, I made the down payment right away. It's something to be proud of, right? However, if everyone did the same, it wouldn't be exceptional. Everyone, whether a basketball player, a footballer, or someone else, wants recognition for their achievements.

Take my friend who owns a weight loss center, for instance. They appreciate acknowledgment for their efforts just like anyone else. When it comes to their homes, they may have appliances or features that are unfamiliar to you, but it's essential to research and appreciate them nonetheless. I once visited a home with solar shingles that cost more than my entire house, and the owners were rightfully proud of it. They don't expect you to match their income or lifestyle; they just want you to be reliable, understanding, and attentive to their needs.

Michael LaFido:

What advice would you have for an agent who's never sold a luxury home but would like to add luxury buyers and sellers to their clientele?

One strategy is to offer to host open houses for fellow agents who are unable to do so themselves. However, it's important to tread carefully, as many luxury clients prefer not to have open houses in their homes. So, to transition into high-end properties and eventually luxury homes, you need to elevate your approach. It's like climbing stairs; you can't reach the top until you take the first step. That's how I started in my neighborhood. Hosting open houses allowed me to familiarize myself with different properties and their selling points.

In Texas, the benchmark for a luxury home is typically around one million dollars, although in areas like Austin, it might be higher. I targeted neighborhoods where homes were valued at over a million dollars. I created pamphlets showcasing my work, including photos of homes I sold and my marketing strategies. Remember those video brochures you showed us? I invested in some and sent them to potential buyers identified through MLS data. This allowed them to see the quality of my work and the properties I represent, even if they didn't feature extravagant features like solar shingles. It's all about highlighting the property's appeal and effective marketing. I highly recommend focusing on... Well, let's just say, targeting specific areas is key.

Michael LaFido:

Well, like a target but focus on?

Lucinda Gadson:

Focus on. I think you did that too. You found a neighborhood that you wanted to go to and you drove over there and you worked in that neighborhood all day long and then you would go home, like going to the office. That's kind of what I did. I highly recommend that you find the neighborhood you want to work in, send them, talk to them, hang out in the coffee shop there, and send postcards, pamphlet type postcards, not just little postcards, high-end postcards or pamphlets. I did the videos in the one million more because I wanted to have the license. It was just a goal for me to have two of them.

Michael LaFido:

What's your approach to say, "All right, unique property, I'm going to have to market this maybe different than an entry level property"? When it comes to marketing the home itself, what recommendations do you have?

Lucinda Gadson:

I follow your teachings closely. My approach is to immerse potential buyers in the lifestyle they could have on a particular property. Let me share a couple of examples. Once, I sold a buffalo ranch, and to showcase its lifestyle, I had drones capturing the scene as GMC Sierra and Dooley trucks drove through the ranch, followed by the wife in her Escalade. I collaborated with local businesses like the Cadillac dealership for the Escalade and the GMC dealership for the trucks. Conveniently, my husband drives a truck, making it effortless to feature a GMC in the footage.

I arranged for the drones to film as they drove past the buffaloes grazing, approached the statue, and explored the hotel on the property. It painted a vivid picture of the recreational activities available, from horseback riding to dirt biking, creating an enticing narrative for potential buyers.

Michael LaFido:

Do you have any insights or successful strategies for reaching out to potential buyers and sellers through different channels? For instance, when you're dealing with properties like the buffalo ranch or one with a creek running through it, do you view each property as a distinct asset? If so, how do you tailor your approach to attract potential buyers for each unique property?

Lucinda Gadson:

Well, regarding the buffalo ranch, I've had a longstanding relationship with the owner spanning about 20 years. It's nestled among a cluster of luxury properties within my network of acquaintances in that area. As for the other property, it was listed by the owner's close friend. I offered some suggestions for marketing improvements, always aiming to add value. I see it as an opportunity to demonstrate my expertise and hopefully forge a connection for potential collaboration down the line. It's not about criticism; it's about offering insights on how to enhance the listing's appeal.

Michael LaFido:

Are you finding success in reaching out to potential high-end sellers who may not currently be on the market, or perhaps had listings that were canceled or expired? What strategies are proving effective for you in today's market, given the shortage of sellers?

Lucinda Gadson:

I've primarily focused on my existing sphere of influence. Given my recent health challenges, I've prioritized reconnecting with my network. Starting with my sphere is beneficial because they tend to be supportive and are more likely to refer me to others. Dealing with for sale by owner properties requires a certain level of readiness and preparation. You need to be well-prepared and have a solid pipeline of potential clients ready to close deals before engaging with them.

Michael LaFido:

Looking ahead, how do you perceive your future trajectory, especially considering the medical setbacks you've faced? With the knowledge and strategies gained from our course and others, including marketing and mindset techniques, how confident do you feel about your prospects in the luxury real estate market? Can you share insights into how your confidence and optimism have been influenced by your certification and hands-on experience in this niche, particularly in terms of showcasing lifestyle and utilizing video marketing?

Lucinda Gadson:

Sitting here and reflecting on our conversation, I realize that everything I've shared aligns perfectly with what I learned in your class. It's like a lightbulb moment—I'm equipped for this. The confidence and knowledge I gained from your course have been invaluable. While I understand that door-to-door approaches aren't everyone's favorite, I feel empowered enough to confidently engage with a stranger about selling their $2.2 million listing home.

Michael LaFido:

It's essential to understand the different price points in the market. There are essentially five categories: starter level, average, high end (twice the market average), luxury (three times the market average), and ultra luxury (ten times the market average). Your position in the luxury category, being in the three times the market average range, is commendable.

Lucinda Gadson:

Yes, indeed. Even in this price range, there are crucial factors to consider. Using high-quality photography is essential; it's a testament to the hard work put into these properties. While some agents may have photography skills, it's crucial to prioritize professional display.

Your class enlightened me on alternative approaches, like reaching out to businesses such as newly opened Mercedes dealerships, fostering partnerships, and referrals. Establishing relationships with businesses like Lexus dealerships and Range Rover sellers nearby has been invaluable. These connections ensure that when they encounter potential clients, you're the first person they think of.

The practical knowledge gained from your class, whether through podcasts or direct instruction, has boosted my confidence and provided me with actionable strategies. It's these insights that make the difference; they empower me to navigate situations effectively and secure listings.

Michael LaFido:

What guidance would you offer to someone who's undecided about pursuing luxury real estate, whether they're a novice or an experienced agent? Perhaps they're facing challenges such as not meeting their brokerage's criteria for their luxury division. Our course, as you're aware, doesn't demand any prior luxury sales for certification, and we offer luxury group coaching. Based on your ex-

perience, do you advise others to invest in a luxury coach or pursue certification? Did you find the return on investment worthwhile?

Lucinda Gadson:

I strongly urge them to pursue this path. Understanding the intricacies of the luxury market, such as the requirements for designations and effectively communicating with affluent clients, is crucial. Without this knowledge, I wouldn't have been able to market and sell high-end properties successfully. Obtaining these designations not only enhances your credibility but also opens doors to lucrative opportunities. Additionally, our course offers Continuing Education credits, which sets it apart from other luxury training programs.

Bonus Section

Tips for Home Sellers

Michael LaFido:

Now, transitioning to our bonus section, tailored for consumers— those who own high-end or luxury properties, whether it's their primary residence or a vacation home. It's essential to recognize that not all agents are equal in expertise and capabilities. When interviewing agents to represent their unique property, what key attributes should these homeowners prioritize? What specific skill sets should they seek? What questions should they ask during the interview process? Could you provide one, two, or even three top tips in this regard?

Lucinda Gadson:

I would advise caution when considering a discount broker. If they're unable to negotiate their own commission, it raises questions about their ability to negotiate effectively on your behalf. Additionally, the quality of photography and presentation of your home is paramount. Ask potential agents how they would showcase another property, even if it's not in the same price range. Look for agents with designations like the Education Deluxe designation; it demonstrates a commitment to ongoing education and expertise in the field. While some individuals may possess innate intelligence, opting for an agent who actively seeks out education shows a dedication to thoroughly researching and marketing every aspect of your home—a crucial factor in achieving a successful sale. That would be my recommendation to any seller.

Tips for Home Buyers

Michael LaFido:

On the other hand, when it comes to purchasing a high-end or luxury property, whether for their primary residence or a vacation home, what qualities should a buyer look for in an agent to help them decide if they should hire that agent and sign A Buyer Representation Agreement with them?

Lucinda Gadson:

Similarly, having the LUXE Designation indicates an agent's commitment to educating themselves about the properties they represent. This means they can provide you with insights beyond just the physical structure of the home, helping you understand the true value of your investment. The key skill here is curiosity—a willingness to delve deeper into the property and its surrounding factors. While agents aren't inspectors or appraisers, their curiosity can lead to a more informed buying experience for you as they uncover essential details about the property.

Visit: SecretsOfTopLuxuryAgents.com
to learn more about Lucinda Gadson

Connect with Lucinda Gadson by Scanning the QR Code Below

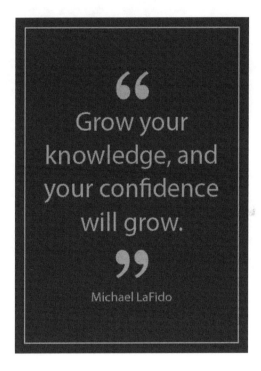

PART 3

SUMMARY AND NEXT STEPS

FREE RESOURCES & DOWNLOADS!

Scan the QR Code For A FREE List Of The Companies We recommend For Website Development, Lead Generation, Prospecting, CRM's, & All Other Services To Help You Become The Leading Luxury Agent In Your Market

Hire Michael To Speak

Michael's speaking engagements cover some of the most up-to-the-minute topics in the luxury real estate market today.

Speaking topics include:

- How To Break Into AND Dominate Listing Higher End Homes In Your Market

- Utilizing Video to Win Over More High End Clients

- How to Host High End Events to Get Luxury Listings Sold

LUXURY SPECIALIST DESIGNATION (LUXE)

24/7 ONLINE ACCESS TO ALL TRAINING AND MATERIALS

Interested in getting certified in luxury? LUXE requires zero previous luxury home sales to get certified in luxury. This course in taught both in person and on demand with a self-paced option through LUXE University. The LUXE Designation establishes a new set of standards for agents. Certified Luxury Agents with the LUXE Designation have been shattering records in their markets and have been increasing their average sales prices. Don't just take our word for it, take a look at all the reviews and case studies.

LUXE requires zero previous luxury sales to take this course and get certified in luxury. LUXE can be taken in person or via an online self-paced course and you have access to all materials online or you can take the class in person. With this Designation, agents have access to proven and repeatable marketing systems, which can be utilized in the marketing of their luxury listings.

To learn more on the LUXE Designation, please visit
LuxeDesignation.com

LUXURY LISTING
SPECIALIST PODCAST

LESSONS LEARNED: A LOOK BACK AT OUR
MOST POPULAR EPISODES!

DOMINATE HIGH END LISTINGS IN ANY MARKET

HOSTED BY MICHAEL LAFIDO
LUXURY REAL ESTATE EXPERT, SPEAKER & TRAINER

EPISODE #300

Want to break into selling high end homes?
Subscribe to the Luxury Listing Specialist Podcast

LuxuryListingPodcast.com

Please leave us a 5 star review if you have learned
something this book or from listening to our Podcast.

ReviewLuxeNow.com

GET YOUR FIRST LUXURY LISTING WITHOUT SPENDING ANY MONEY ON MARKETING

Are you ready to break into the world of luxury real estate without breaking the bank?

- Expert Insights & Proven Strategies

- Maximize Success, Minimize Investment

- Immediate Impact With Actionable Steps

- How To Build Connections & Expand Your Network

*Get it **NOW** at*

LuxuryListingBlueprint.com

NEED SOME LUXURY SWAG?

Check Out our gear at

LuxurySpecialistGear.com

LUXURY COACHING WITH MICHAEL LAFIDO

Interested in taking your business to the next level?

Scan The QR Code To Find Out More About

Luxury Coaching With Michael LaFido

Join Our LUXE Community

Scan the QR code to join our community.

When you join, please take a picture of yourself holding up this book, and post that picture in our group introducing yourself to our group and your biggest "ah-ha" takeaway from this book. Use the hashtag #Luxury-ListingSpecialist in the post.

Thanks again for investing in yourself with the purchase of this book. I can't wait to hear about your success story.

SUMMARY, IMPLEMENTATION & ACTION STEPS

As you finish this book, my goal was to motivate and inspire you to take action to attract more opportunities and to sell more high-end and luxury homes in your market. It is possible when you implement the information you've learned throughout each of the chapters.

I know that it is not easy to stay motivated, to build and or grow your real estate business profitably while still maintaining your sanity, health, marriage, relationship with your kids, work/life balance, and having a happy and sound spiritual life.

But it's entirely possible. We have shared tons of secrets and golden nuggets to help you take a few shortcuts that will get you immediate results and help you increase your average sales price and earn more money this year without spending all the time and effort it normally requires agents to break into or dominate selling luxury homes.

If you've enjoyed and learned from what you've read (or most of what you've read), I would absolutely love to hear from you and get to know you better. I would also appreciate you posting a success story, picture, or video, and comment on Amazon, Google or at www.facebook.com/groups/luxurylisting.

I hope our insights have been valuable to you. I'm passionate about luxury real estate, elevating industry standards, and promoting diversity within it. We were intentional to include diversity in this book, ensuring representation from various backgrounds and perspectives. Your feedback is appreciated. If you've found value in this book please leave the book a review on amazon and keep us posted on all your successes!

Michael LaFido

Michael LaFido Founder & CEO
E: Michael@MarketingLuxuryGroup.com

"I'll find out when the power's coming back on. We'll need to push Jas and Noelle's party back until it does."

"I'll take care of it." Lex cradled her wrist, rubbing it gently, as if to erase his touch. "I always do, don't I?"

"You always do," he agreed, closing his hand around empty air. The harder he clutched at her, the faster she slipped away. It had always been true, but it had gotten worse since she'd been shot. Money could buy regenerative technology that healed flesh, but nothing could rid him of the image of her bleeding out on the club's stage.

He couldn't stop tightening his fists, even when he threatened to crush her.

Coming in early 2013

22417157R10200

Made in the USA
San Bernardino, CA
06 July 2015